Wonders
of the
Greek Islands

The Cyclades

DENIS ROUBIEN

ii

This book is dedicated to those who accompanied me
in the exploration of these treasure islands

CONTENTS

1 ANDROS. THE LITTLE ENGLAND OF THE CYCLADES

Andros. An English countryside in the Cyclades. Hiking from Apikia to Pythara

Pythara. Waterfalls in the Cyclades!

Andros was known in the past as 'Little England' because of its naval force, which sealed its history and, along with it, its physiognomy. The ship-owners of Andros had their offices in England, had brought English furniture to their fine mansions and had even adopted English habits, like the ritual of afternoon tea. However, if you go for hiking in its hinterland in the spring, you will feel that this nickname also fits well its countryside. Maybe nowhere else in the Cyclades will you feel so surprised by the quantity of water and greenery you will find. If we add to this a capital constituting one of the finest neoclassical ensembles in Greece and a significant number of monuments of all times, Andros is definitely a destination worth putting into your programme.

Our first hike (always the well-known group, under the guidance of Kostas) was from Apikia to Pythara where we saw waterfalls. Yes, waterfalls in the Cyclades! And they would not be the only ones! The route predisposes you to the beauty you will face in the 'Fairyland' as the folk tradition calls it.

From Apikia to Stenies and to Gialia

The tower of Bistis - Mouvelas as seen on the route from Apikia to Stenies

Our next hike was from Apikia to Stenies, and from there to Gialia.

On the way, we passed from the tower of Bistis - Mouvelas, near Stenies. In the countryside of Andros, there are various tower houses of squires, dating from the 17th to the 19th century. They are tall square fortified towers. Access was a mobile staircase and an elevated window. The oldest such structure is the three-storey tower of Bistis-Mouvelas.

The tower was built by Stamatelos Bistis towards the end of the 17th century, sometime after 1674 and certainly before 1696, when it's certain that Bistis was already inhabiting it. Chora (the capital) was looted in 1674 by pirates, and the rulers of the island were seeking at that time more security in the hinterland. 'Mouvelas' was a nickname of Bistis and means the surrogate of the cadi (Turkish judge).

Three building phases are identified in the tower. The first one dates probably from the 13th century since the building we see was built on the ruins of a square medieval tower.

At the 'Fabrica' of Embirikos

The Fabrika of Embirikos as we saw it as we were arriving from the trail

Then we arrived at Embirikos's 'Fabrica'. The Embirikos Mill is an interesting combination of steam and watermill and a rare remnant of the first phase of industrialization in Greece. The 'Fabrica', as the complex is known, is located at Pera Panta, under Stenies. Its five buildings are arranged on rocky ground with great inclination, next to the riverbed, amidst lush vegetation.

The watermill was built in 1876 by Konstantinos Embirikos. He made a large flour mill for processing the wheat he imported with his own ships from Romania. The products were flour and packaged flour products, but it's not known whether they were intended for the domestic market alone or whether they were also being exported. The seamen of Andros worked in the mill as maintenance engineers when they didn't travel. The factory operated six days a week.

The Mill of Embirikos introduced the industrial production of wheat products on the island with its numerous traditional watermills. On the one hand, it contributed to the overall increase in production, but on the other hand, it caused many small mills to be abandoned.

The 'Fabrika' operated successfully until the early 1930s when competition from the Syros and Piraeus mills increased. Also, the absence of a roadway made transport extremely difficult. It's also said that the coke that burned for the boiler made the operation financially unprofitable. All this led to the decline and eventually the closure of the factory.

At an unknown time, the property passed from the Embirikos family to the other great family of ship-owners, the Goulandris. According to testimonies, this happened because Konstantinos Embirikos pledged the Fabrica to buy boats without eventually succeeding in paying the debt.

At the castle of Faneromeni

We found ourselves at the castle of Faneromeni following the trail Kochylou - Faneromeni Castle - Dipotamata - Syneti. The Castle of Faneromeni or Apano Kastro (Upper Castle) or Grias Kastro (the castle of the old woman) was the largest medieval city of Andros (but there are also traces of a Roman fortification). It was built by the Venetians for protection against pirates. Remains of houses, aqueducts and walls are still preserved.

Many legends are associated with this castle. Most have an old woman as a protagonist, who either betrayed or wanted to warn or attempted to escape. Whatever it is, the memory of the old woman has been engraved and a little farther it has given its name to the famous beach of 'tis grias to pidima' (the jump of the old woman).

The castle of Faneromeni. In the foreground, we see two of the many 'katikies' of the Cycladic countryside. They are small constructions of dry stone, namely, without mortar. The farmers used them in times when travel was difficult. When they had a lot of work, they had no time to return to their village every night. So, they were staying here

At Dipotamata

The huge local slabs of shale, typical of Andros, determine the forms of traditional architecture, adapted to the island's climate and materials. Additionally, the use of local materials made the settlements invisible at a distance in the time of piracy

Then our route brought us to Dipotamata (double river). It's one of the most beautiful places on the island, a terrestrial paradise with lavish vegetation, old watermills (22 are preserved) and stone bridges.

The very characteristic dry stone walls of Andros, different from those of other islands. Huge local slabs interrupt harmonically at intervals the construction of smaller stones

At the noble Chora

Then, the programme had a visit to Chora, one of Greece's finest neoclassical ensembles. The result, of course, of the wealth that shipping has brought to the island and gave it the nickname 'Little England'. When Greece became an independent state in 1830, classicism was supposed to form the link with the ancient past. Therefore, public buildings were made according to this style and the upper classes adopted it with enthusiasm in their mansions. The wealthy ship-owners of Andros were among them.

On the other hand, the rest of the population usually integrated some characteristic elements into the insisting traditional architecture, which was better adapted to the country's climate conditions and the owners' financial means. That explains why in the rest of the Cyclades (apart from Syros, the other island of ship-owners), traditional architecture prevails.

The present settlement is an extension of the much smaller medieval settlement. It was built by the Venetians who, under the direction of Marino Dandolo, conquered Andros in 1207. Since then, Andros has been part of the Duchy of the Archipelago, which was based in Naxos and lasted until the death of the last duke in 1566. Then all the islands except Tinos were officially incorporated into the Ottoman Empire, which had in fact conquered them in 1537, leaving however the duke in his place.

Marino Dandolo also built the castle on the islet on the edge of the peninsula, known as 'Kato Kastro' (lower castle), as opposed to 'Apano Kastro' (upper castle), the castle of Faneromeni. Inside the castle lived the governor of the island with his guard and here the inhabitants of Chora took refuge in case of a raid. The Venitians also built the Catholic cathedral of Saint Andew, which exists until today.

Chora with its ruined castle on the islet. The medieval settlement was right on the edge of the peninsula. In the event of a raid, the inhabitants passed from the small bridge to the castle, on the islet. There it was easier to confront the enemies

The capital of Andros (Chora) is one of Greece's finest neoclassical ensembles. The result of the wealth that shipping has brought to the island and gave it the nickname 'Little England'

The seal of ship-owners is everywhere, since they have funded all charitable foundations: Here, the hospital-nursing home founded by the Embirikos

A memory from the traditional architecture: a sahnisin (closed balcony) in a neoclassical house where there should normally be a marble balcony

The Kampanis fountain in Kairis Square. The priest and philosopher Theophilos Kairis (1784-1853) is one of the most famous children of Andros. Behind it, the Archaeological Museum, founded with a donation of Basil and Elise Goulandris Foundation

In Kairis Square, you can visit the Archaeological Museum, with interesting exhibits from the island's rich history, from the Prehistoric period until recently. Although few things have been discovered about prehistoric Andros, the Cyclades occupied a prominent position in Prehistory, thanks to their central location in the Aegean Sea. The islands of the Aegean acted as a bridge uniting Europe to Asia and profited from the commercial activities between these lands, their ports receiving the ships which ensured that trade. The 3rd millennium BC, i.e. the Early Bronze Age, was the era of the so-called Cycladic civilization, which created the world-famous astonishing Cycladic figurines. These works of art in local white marble impress by their abstract forms, which inspired many modern artists. At that time the Cyclades had a dense population, installed in small settlements along the islands' coasts.

However, the settlements of the Cycladic civilization had a violent end, which resulted in the interruption of this artistic creation. Around 2000 BC, the Cyclades started being influenced by the Minoan civilization of Crete, the new emerging power in the Aegean Sea. That led to a new period of prosperity in the Cyclades, which ended with the decline of Crete around 1500 BC and the arrival of the Mycenaeans, who dominated the last phase of Bronze Age in Greece (Mycenaean period, 1600-1100 BC).

The Geometric period (900-700 BC) followed the two centuries of chaos engendered by the arrival of the Dorians in about 1100 BC and the subsequent fall of the Mycenaean civilization. Andros is now mainly inhabited by Ionians who came from Attica.

In the Archaic period (7th – 6th century BC), which followed the Geometric period, the Cyclades experienced a new era of prosperity. In the Classical period all the Cyclades declined with the rise of Athens in the 5th century BC and their compulsory adhesion to the Athenian Alliance, which transformed them into Athens's satellites.

The most impressive exhibit is the famous statue of Hermes of Andros. It dates from the 1st century BC and is a marble copy of a bronze statue by Praxiteles, of about 350 BC. It shows Hermes with a cloak slung over his left shoulder. Although he lacks the traditional attributes of the god (the winged sandals and wand or caduceus), this may be due to damage: the arms are missing and the lower legs are restorations. One of the two snakes that normally coil around Hermes's wand is now on the tree-trunk support.

The statue was found in 1832 in Paleopolis, at the island's western coast, where the ancient city of Andros was situated. Dimitrios Loukrezis, digging his field, found two statues, both of Parian marble, one in the form of a naked young man and the second, a female figure in a tunic and robe. This discovery made sense, despite the fact that the inhabitants of Paleopolis often found antiquities in the area occupied by the ancient city of Andros.

King Otto himself, during his visit to Andros, was impressed by the sculpture, paid to Loukrezis the amount of 6 drachmas and ordered its transfer to Athens, in order to donate the masterpiece to the newly established National Archaeological Museum that was still housed in the temple of Hephaestus, the so-called Theseion, in the Ancient Agora. The Bavarian King Otto offered to send Loukrezis's son to Germany to study, but he was limited to the money.

Hermes of Andros. Photo by Zde / CC BY-SA
https://creativecommons.org/licenses/by-sa/3.0)

Behind the Archaeological Museum, you can visit the Museum of Contemporary Art, founded by Basil and Elise Goulandris Foundation and based on the private collection of the homonymous couple. It is astonishingly rich for the island's size, with one of the most important art collections in Greece. It contains more than 300 works of world-famous artists. Moreover, it organizes temporary exhibitions of artists like Pablo Picasso, Henri Matisse, Wassily Kandinsky, Balthus, Alberto Giacometti, Paul Klee, Marc Chagall, Giorgio de Chirico, Auguste Rodin, Camille Claudel, Henry Moore, Edgar Degas, Paul Cézanne.

Riva Square. The statue of the Disappeared Sailor, in honour of all sailors who lost their lives at sea. It's the work of Michael Tombros (1889-1974)

The few remaining ruins of the medieval castle. It was destroyed in 1943 by a German bombardment. The connection point of its islet with the settlement

At the monasteries of Andros

Andros also has very important monasteries. We visited three of them. We started with the abandoned monastery of Saint Irene, near Apikia, dating from 1780. Then we visited the equally abandoned monastery of Saint Nicholas, also near Apikia. Possible date of construction is considered to be 1540.

From the Mesaria valley, we started the long hiking that led us to the Panachrantos (Immaculate Virgin Mary) monastery. Following an upward course, we reached the inhabited monastery of Panachrantos. The monastery was founded by Nikephoros Phocas as a sign of gratitude for the liberation of Crete from the Arabs in 961. However, today's buildings are the result of later rebuilding. Here we ate pasta prepared under the supervision of the abbot, Father Evdokimos.

The monastery of Saint Marina, near Apikia, as seen from Chora. The fortified aspect is due to the dangers of piracy

Monastery of Saint Irene

The entrance of the monastery of Saint Nicholas, with the alternation of white and green stone, reminds intensely of the Tuscan churches in Italy. Long-standing Venetian domination can explain these influences. The contrast between 'official' styles and anonymous traditional architecture couldn't be greater

The church of the monastery of Saint Nicholas presents Italian influences similar to those of the monastery's entrance

Ruined medieval settlement in the valley of Mesaria

The roof of a chapel in the valley of Mesaria. The huge slabs are typical of Andros, as of neighbouring Tinos, the two islands being geologically related

Monastery of Panachrantos. Here also, the fortified aspect is due to the dangers of piracy

Lardia - Rogo - Ormos Korthiou

The trail Lardia - Rogo - Ormos Korthiou (Bay of Korthi) was the next one in the programme. Here, one can meet villages which have preserved their medieval form, from the time of the Venetian domination (1207-1566), and which are very different from the villages of the ship-owners, where the neoclassical architecture that transformed them after 1830 made their initial form disappear. In these villages, for protection against pirates, the locals built their houses attached to one another. Thus, they formed a continuous outer front, with no openings, like a fortification. Of course, after the end of piracy, openings were created and other houses added, less densely placed around the medieval core, which sometimes makes it difficult to distinguish the oldest parts of these villages.

Above, a village which preserves its dense medieval form, for the protection of the inhabitants against pirates. Below, a dovecote next to Ormos Korthiou

Ormos Korthiou. Tis Grias to Pidima (the old woman's jump). Here, according to the legend, the old woman who betrayed or wanted to escape from the Upper Castle (Faneromeni or Grias Castle) fell and was transformed into this rock

Menites - Lamyra – Chora

The next trail, Menites - Lamyra - Chora, was also in an idyllic setting, which was nothing like the characteristic dry Cycladic landscape.

About the name of the village of Menites, there is the view that it derives from the mainads, the nymphs of Dionysus, but another version claims that the name Mainites comes from the Latin word 'amoenitas', meaning a pleasant place.

Mesaria – Chora

On the trail from Mesaria to Chora, we met the important 12th century Byzantine church of Taxiarchis (Saint Michael).

And here we finished our trip, full of the images of this indescribable beauty we gathered in just three days. And think that we didn't get to visit any of the great museums that this culturally so rich island has. But next time...

Menites

Mesaria. The 12th-century Byzantine church of Taxiarchis (Saint Michael)

2 MILOS. THE FLOATING WONDER OF THE AEGEAN

Milos. A floating geological wonder

You have arrived at Milos? Go immediately and take one of the ships that make the tour of the island. Because, if it gets windy and you don't make the sea tour, you lost! You didn't see anything.

Because Milos has, of course, all the beauties that you expect to find in a Cycladic island. In this, it will not disappoint you at all. But apart from that, it also has something unique. Due to its volcanic origin, it's a floating geological wonder: it has coasts of unique geological wealth, a unique landscape variety. And most points are only accessible by sea. So, get started immediately. And you will see the following wonders, in the order that the ships going around the island encounter them.

Kleftiko. The base of pirates

Kleftiko includes probably the most famous images of Milos. Words are needless. Here goes more than ever 'a picture is worth a thousand words'. In its countless caves, it once hid pirates, that's why it was named so (kleftis meaning thief in Greek). Today it's a shelter for yachts. Don't omit to dive from the ship. Preferably with a mask. You will understand why...

Glaronisia (islands of the seagulls). Some of the strangest geological formations in Milos

Sarakiniko. When the Moon fell into the Aegean

And the ship reaches the second most well-known image of Milos after Kleftiko: Sarakiniko. Also this name suggests it was a pirates' shelter (Sarakinos meaning Saracen). However, unlike Kleftiko, it's also accessible by land. But you must also see it from the sea. You will think you are on the Moon, but on a Moon with water.

photo by Denis Roubien

The 'syrmata'

As the tour of Milos approaches its end, you will see the 'syrmata'. They are old fishermen's dwellings (on the upper floor), with space for the boat on the ground floor. Today, of course, they are rented to tourists. Their back is dug into the soft volcanic rock. The multicoloured image of the clusters of syrmata is also among the most characteristic ones of Milos.

Fyropotamos. A settlement of 'syrmata'

Arkoudes (Bears). Another unique geological formation

Klima (Vine). The city of Aphrodite

The last stop before the tour of the island is completed is at Klima (Vine). Here you will see the largest set of syrmata, beneath Plaka, the capital of Milos.

But in Klima was also the island's ancient capital, which was built by the Dorians and replaced the prehistoric Phylakopi after its abandonment in 1100 BC. Many ancient ruins lie here, especially a well-preserved Roman theatre. Also here was found the famous Aphrodite of Milos, currently at the Louvre Museum in Paris.

Aphrodite of Milos, better known as the Venus de Milo, is an ancient Greek statue and one of the most famous works of ancient Greek sculpture. Initially it was attributed to the sculptor Praxiteles. However, from an inscription that was on its plinth, the statue is thought to be the work of Alexander of Antioch. Created sometime between 130 and 100 BC, the statue is believed to depict Aphrodite, the Greek goddess of love and beauty (Venus to the Romans). It is a marble sculpture, slightly larger than life size, 203 cm high.

It was found mutilated and the goddess held in her left hand an apple or a mirror, or she held the shield of Mars with both hands. Others think that she was ready to bathe. About her arms there is a myth that they broke at the scuffle between French archaeologists and Greeks during the transfer of the statue, but that is not true because the work had been found from the beginning without arms.

What is probably true is that parts of the arms were found in different places, and that the left hand held an apple but was lost during transport or that, during the scuffle (which actually took place in order to acquire it), some of the pieces that accompanied the sculpture (like the left hand) fell into the sea from the rocks and were lost forever.

It is generally asserted that the Aphrodite of Milos was discovered on 8 April 1820, when the island was a part of the Ottoman Empire, by a peasant named George Kentrotas, inside a buried niche within the ruins of the ancient city of Milos.

Elsewhere the discoverers are identified as George Bottonis and his son Anthony. Paul Carus describes the site of discovery as 'the ruins of an ancient theatre in the vicinity of Kastro, the island's capital', adding that Bottonis and his son 'came accidentally across a small cave, carefully covered with a heavy slab and concealed, which contained a fine marble statue in two pieces, along with several other marble fragments. This happened in February, 1820'. Apparently, he based these assertions on an article he had read in the *Century Magazine*.

The Australian historian Edward Duyker, citing a letter written by Louis Brest, the French consul in Milos in 1820, asserts the discoverer of the statue was Theodore Kentrotas, confused with his younger son George who later claimed credit for the find. Duyker asserts that Kentrotas was taking stones from a ruined chapel on the edge of his property – terraced land that had once formed part of a Roman gymnasium – and that he discovered an oblong cavity in the volcanic tuff. It was in this cavity, which had three wings, that Kentrotas first noticed the upper part of the statue.

What is certain is that the statue was found in two large pieces (the upper torso and the lower draped legs) along with several herms (pillars topped with heads), fragments of the upper left arm and left hand holding an apple, and an inscribed plinth, also lost.

Aphrodite of Milos. Photo by Mattgirling [CC BY-SA 3.0 (https://creativecommons.org/licenses/by-sa/3.0)

The 'syrmata' of Klima

Adamas. The overlooked

And now that you have made the sea tour, it's time to discover Milos by land. The ship will bring you back to Adamas, the starting point.

Don't make the mistake to be misled by the view of the harbour and ignore it. The old village, more to the back, is worthy of the Cyclades and is definitely worth a visit.

At the edge of the harbour, do not omit to visit the exemplary and extremely interesting Mining Museum. Such a museum is really necessary in this geological wonder of the Aegean.

The omissions of the trip. Phylakopi and Papafragas

If you advance in the hinterland, you will see two places that you saw from afar, circumnavigating the island, but didn't notice them, because they are not visible from a distance.

One is the ancient city of Phylakopi, which was mentioned before. It's one of the most important prehistoric archaeological sites in Greece. Its remains cover the entire Bronze Age (3000-1100 BC). It was built on the island's northern coast, so as to permit surveillance of a big part of the sea.

The Cyclades occupied a prominent position in Prehistory, thanks to their central location in the Aegean Sea. The islands of the Aegean acted as a bridge uniting Europe to Asia and profited from the commercial activities between these lands, their ports receiving the ships which ensured that trade. The 3rd millennium BC, i.e. the Early Bronze Age, was the era of the so-called Cycladic civilization, which created the world-famous astonishing Cycladic figurines. These works of art in local white marble impress by their abstract forms, which inspired many modern artists. At that time the Cyclades had a dense population, installed in small settlements along the islands' coasts and Milos experienced a particular prosperity.

However, the settlements of the Cycladic civilization had a violent end, which resulted in the interruption of this artistic creation. Around 2000 BC, the Cyclades started being influenced by the Minoan civilization of Crete, the new emerging power in the Aegean Sea. That led to a new period of prosperity in the Cyclades, which ended with the decline of Crete around 1500 BC and the arrival of the Mycenaeans, who dominated the last phase of Bronze Age in Greece (Mycenaean period, 1600-1100 BC), until the arrival of the Dorians, who put an end to the Mycenaean civilization.

Thanks to the trade of the opsidian, a stone from which many prehistoric tools were made (obsidian is a naturally occurring volcanic glass formed as an extrusive igneous rock), Phylakopi developed into a significant commercial and cultural centre, with Cyclopean walls. It was destroyed and rebuilt three times and definitely abandoned in 1100 BC, with the arrival of the Dorians, who colonized Milos and built the capital we saw in Klima. Today, the city's largest part lies under the surface of the sea, but you can still see the walls, the sanctuary and the palace. There is also a very interesting museum, with findings of extreme archaeological importance.

The other point that is not well visible during the sea tour is Papafragas. It's a sea cave, named after a Catholic priest (papas = priest, Fragos = Frank = Catholic for medieval Greeks) who kept his boat here. If there is no North wind, you can swim.

The ruins of Phylakopi, on the edge of the cliff. Half of the city has submerged into the sea

Plaka. The ideal end of the island's tours

The ideal place to end your tours in Milos is the island's capital, Plaka.

On the one hand, because most of the best restaurants, cafes and bars are concentrated here so that you can relax from the all-day tour or from the sea baths under the relentless sun of the Cyclades.

On the other hand, because here you will see the most beautiful sunset of Milos.

Also nearby, in the neighbouring village of Trypiti, are the famous Early Christian catacombs. They are unique in size throughout Greece and perhaps the oldest Christian monument in the world since they date back to the 2nd century AD. They were the first gathering place of the first Christians and they were used as a municipal cemetery for the first time in the end of the 2nd century BC.

But everything was buried under huge volumes of rocks after the earthquakes of the 6th century AD and became a legend throughout the centuries. Until 1843, when the first descent to the monument was made by the German professor of archaeology Ludwig Ross, who rushed in as soon as the entrance was discovered. But he realised that thieves had preceded him...

The catacombs of Milos. Photo by Vihou World / CC BY-SA
(https://creativecommons.org/licenses/by-sa/4.0)

The catacombs of Milos. Photo by Klearchos Kapoutsis from Santorini, Greece /
CC BY (https://creativecommons.org/licenses/by/2.0)

The Archaeological Museum of Milos. A neodassical 'dissonance' among the typical Cydadic traditional architecture. When Greece became an independent State in 1830, dassicism was supposed to form the link with the ancient past. Therefore, public buildings were made according to this style and the upper dasses adopted it with enthusiasm in their mansions. On the other hand, the rest of the population usually integrated some characteristic elements into the insisting traditional architecture, which was better adapted to the country's dimate conditions and the owners' financial means. Since the Cydades were islands of particularly restricted wealth, here neodassical architecture was usually limited to public structures and very few houses of the most wealthy citizens. The exceptions were the islands of the ship-owners, Syros and Andros

photo by Denis Roubien

The Catholic church of the Virgin Mary of the Roses. Milos, like most islands of the Cyclades, has a Catholic community, due to the long Venetian domination, a result of the 4th crusade. The Venetian domination lasted from 1207 to 1566. During this period, Milos has been part of the Duchy of the Archipelago, founded by the Venetian nobleman Marco Sanudo, with Naxos as its capital. In 1566 the Cyclades were officially incorporated into the Ottoman Empire.; which had in fact already conquered them since 1537, but leaving the Duke in his place

photo by Denis Roubien

Part of the house is above the street, as an elegant solution to the lack of space in the medieval settlements of the Aegean. Due to the threat of pirates, the settlements were fortified, which led to the concentration of the population within a very limited space. That, in its turn, led to these arched passages, so characteristic of these settlements

At the time of piracy, houses didn't have any external staircases, for safety reasons, and the two floors communicated through an internal steep wooden ladder. When piracy was eliminated, after the creation of the new Greek State in 1830, the lack of space led to this solution, in order to link externally the two floors

photo by Denis Roubien

As you have seen, Milos has everything you expect from a Cycladic island, but also much more. So, if you haven't visited it, you must put it high in your priorities.

3 MYKONOS – DELOS. THE ANCIENT AND MODERN MEDITERRANEAN HUB

Mykonos. From oblivion to world fame

Mykonos is said to have been the location of the Gigantomachy, the great battle between Zeus and the Giants. According to myth, the large rocks all over the island are said to be the petrified corpses of the Giants.

The Cyclades occupied a prominent position in Prehistory, thanks to their central location in the Aegean Sea. The islands of the Aegean acted as a bridge uniting Europe to Asia and profited from the commercial activities between these lands, their ports receiving the ships which ensured that trade. The 3rd millennium BC, i.e. the Early Bronze Age, was the era of the so-called Cycladic civilization, which created the world-famous astonishing Cycladic figurines. These works of art in local white marble impress by their abstract forms, which inspired many modern artists. At that time the Cyclades had a dense population, installed in small settlements along the islands' coasts. However, Mykonos doesn't seem to have experienced a particular prosperity, at least according to the archaeological findings to-date.

The settlements of the Cycladic civilization had a violent end, which resulted in the interruption of this artistic creation. Around 2000 BC, the Cyclades started being influenced by the Minoan civilization of Crete, the new emerging power in the Aegean Sea. That led to a new period of prosperity in the Cyclades, which ended with the decline of Crete around 1500 BC and the arrival of the Mycenaeans, who dominated the last phase of Bronze Age in Greece (Mycenaean period, 1600-1100 BC).

The Geometric period (900-700 BC) followed the two centuries of chaos engendered by the arrival of the Dorians in about 1100 BC and the subsequent fall of the Mycenaean civilization. Mykonos is now mainly inhabited by Ionians who came from Attica.

In the Archaic period (7th – 6th century BC), which followed the Geometric period, some islands experienced a new era of prosperity, but Mykonos was not among them. Ancient writers almost always mention it with contempt on account of its poverty and insignificance. The island's poverty accounts for the reputation of ancient Mykonians as mean people and parasites. There was even the expression 'Mykonian neighbour' which meant the uninvited guest.

In the Classical period all the Cyclades declined with the rise of Athens in the 5th century BC and their compulsory adhesion to the Athenian Alliance, which transformed them into Athens's satellites.

Mykonos came under the control of the Romans and then became part of the Byzantine Empire until the 12th century. In 1207, three years after the crusaders of the 4th crusade conquered the Byzantine Empire, Marco Sanudo, a Venetian nobleman, nephew of the doge Enrico Dandolo, seized most of the Cyclades. He created the Duchy of the Archipelago and settled in Naxos. Tinos and Mykonos, however, were not part of this State. That same year they came under the two Venetian brothers Andrea and Geremia Ghisi and their heirs. That lasted until 1390 when Venice undertook their direct administration.

In 1537, Mykonos was conquered by Hayreddin Barbarossa, the admiral of the Ottoman sultan Suleiman the Magnificent. Like in the rest of the Cyclades, the Ottomans never established themselves in these islands, which didn't interest them because of their poverty. This is why there is no trace of their passage.

Contrary to other islands of the Aegean which suffered from the pirates, Mykonos was one of their shelters and its inhabitants exercised an extensive trade with them. From the end of the 17th century, Mykonos started becoming a naval power. Up until the end of the 18th century, it prospered as a trading centre, attracting many immigrants from nearby islands, in addition to regular pirate raids. During the Napoleonic Wars, the Mykonians provided with cereals the blocked populations, thus gaining both material means and naval experience, which proved very useful a little later, in the Greek Revolution.

The Greek Revolution against the Ottoman Empire broke out in 1821 and Mykonos with its fleet played an important role, led by the national heroine, Manto Mavrogenous. This great personality of modern Greek history, a well-educated aristocrat guided by the ideas of the Enlightenment, sacrificed her family's fortune for the Greek cause.

As a result of sailing and merchant activity, the island's economy quickly picked up but declined again during the late 19th century and especially after the opening of the Corinth Canal in 1893 and World War I. Since the 1960's, tourism came to dominate the local economy, owing a lot to the important excavations carried out by the French School of Archaeology in the nearby island of Delos since 1873. From then on, the fate of Mykonos has been the exact opposite of its humble ancient history.

Chora. The archetypal Greek island settlement

Chora, the capital of Mykonos, could be called the most typical Greek island settlement. Despite the very intense tourist activity, it has surprisingly maintained its beauty and characteristic picturesque image with its small whitewashed houses and churches, the wooden balconies, bougainvilleas and multi-coloured details. Its narrow winding streets with the continuous front of houses give the impression of being in an interior space.

Chora, the only village proper of Mykonos

Some of Mykonos's famous windmills in Chora, the island's capital. The presence of so many for an island of a relatively small population and, moreover, very arid to produce so many cereals for all these mills to be necessary, is explained by the fact that Mykonos is in a strategic point, a passage between continental Greece and Asia Minor. Its inhabitants bought cereals from other places, made flour in their mills and produced rusks, which they sold to the ships passing through Mykonos's port. Rusks were a basic part of the seamen's diet, due to their ability to be stored for a long time

Little Venice is a block of captains' houses in Chora, dating mainly from the 18th century, time of maximum prosperity of Mykonos's naval activity. It owes its name to the houses being built just above the water, with their lower level communicating with the sea. It is said that in the time of piracy, their owners received from the pirates through the doors at sea level boats charged with valuable objects, which, later, emerged from the house's front part. The first money laundering?

Panaghia Paraportiani (Our Lady of the Side Gate, or Virgin Mary Standing Next to the Entrance Door) is –justly- the most famous church in Mykonos. Situated in the neighbourhood of Kastro (Castle) overlooking the Aegean Sea, it is in fact a complex of many churches that impresses with its plasticity and unique shape, a true sculpture of stones and lime. Panaghia Paraportiani is certainly one of the finest examples of Cycladic architecture and one of the most photographed churches in the world, classified as a National Monument. The complex has its entrance in the side gate of the Kastro neighbourhood (hence, the name). At the lower level there are four churches: the oldest one is that of Saints Anarghyri (Cosma and Damian), dating from the end of the 14th to the beginning of the 15th century. The others are those of Saint Eustace, Saint Sozon and Saint Anastasia. The church of the Virgin Mary is above that of Saint Eustace and gives the whole complex its name

Mykonos has a surprisingly large number of churches. Many of them are private and were built by seamen as a result of their gratitude in case they survived a storm or a pirate attack. A characteristic feature of many of them, different from the churches of other Cycladic islands is the red dome, instead of a blue one, the so typical image of the Greek islands

The existence of more than one church in a row is very common in Mykonos

These houses form part of Kastro (Castle), the oldest neighbourhood of Chora. It dates from the time of Venetian domination, although today's buildings are more recent and gradually replaced the original ones, keeping, though, a large part of that time's layout. For protection against pirates, the locals built their houses attached to one another. Thus, they formed a continuous outer front, with no openings, like a fortification. At that time, houses didn't have any external staircases, for safety reasons, and the two floors communicated through an internal steep wooden ladder. The houses obtained an external staircase only when piracy was eliminated, after the creation of the new Greek State in 1830

Mykonos is the only Cycladic island where we can see these wooden extensions of houses, at least in such a number. The usual method of gaining space in the limited area of the fortified medieval settlements of the Aegean was building a part of the house above the street, in the same materials as the main construction, namely, stone. However, here we see a method more common in the mainland and in the islands of Northern Aegean, where wood was less scarce

The scarcity of space in the fortified medieval settlements made such interventions in the buildings' angles necessary, in order to permit the passage of loaded mules

The landscape of Mykonos is particularly arid, now dotted with tourist developments

Ano Mera is the only other settlement of Mykonos, apart from tourist developments, and still not a village proper, Chora being the only one on the island. It was created around the monastery of Panaghia Tourliani (Virgin Mary of Tourlos). This was founded in 1542 by monks who came from Paros and was initially dedicated to the Presentation of the Virgin Mary. The monastery was restored in 1767 and took its present name after an icon of the Virgin Mary found in the nearby area of Tourlos. Since then, Panaghia Tourliani became the patroness of the island and is celebrated on August, 15th (Assumption of the Virgin Mary).

Ano Mera, monastery of Panaghia Tourliani

Delos. The silent birthplace of Apollo

From Mykonos, you can make a one-day excursion to Delos. This tiny uninhabited island is one of the most important mythological, historical, and archaeological sites in Greece. The excavations in Delos are among the most extensive in the Mediterranean and take place under the direction of the French School at Athens. Many of the findings are displayed at the Archaeological Museum of Delos and the National Archaeological Museum of Athens.

Delos was already a holy sanctuary for an entire millennium before Greek mythology made of it the birthplace of Apollo and Artemis. The discovery of ancient stone huts on the island indicates that it has been inhabited since the 3rd millennium BC. Thucydides mentions that the first inhabitants were Carian pirates who were eventually expelled by King Minos of Crete. According to the Odyssey, the island was already famous as the birthplace of the twin gods Apollo and Artemis.

Between 900 BC and 100 AD, Delos was a major religious centre where also Dionysus and Titaness Leto, mother of Apollo and Artemis, were worshiped. Before becoming a Panhellenic cult centre, Delos was a religious pilgrimage for the Ionians. A number of 'purifications' were performed by the Athenians in order to make the island fit for the worship of the gods. The first took place in the 6th century BC and was ordered by the tyrant Pisistratus. All graves within sight of the temple were dug up and the bodies transferred to Rhenia, a nearby island, also uninhabited today. In the 5th century BC, during the 6th year of the Peloponnesian War, the entire island was purged of all graves, after this was ordered by the Oracle of Delphi. It was then forbidden to die or give birth on the island, ostentatiously because of its sacred importance, but also in order to preserve its neutrality in commerce, since no one could then claim ownership through inheritance. Immediately after this purification, the first quinquennial festival of the Delian games was celebrated there. Four years later, all the inhabitants were transferred to Adramyttium in Asia Minor as a further purification.

After the Persian Wars the island became the meeting place for the Delian League, founded in 478 BC. The meetings were held in the temple of Apollo. The League's common treasury was also kept here until 454 BC when Pericles removed it to Athens, on the pretext of guarding it more safely, but in fact to use it for the construction of the marble temples of the Acropolis. The island didn't produce anything and all necessary products were imported. The very scarce water was exploited through an extensive cistern and aqueduct system, wells, and sanitary drains. Various regions of the Mediterranean operated separate agoras (markets).

According to Strabo, in 166 BC the Romans converted Delos into a free port. This was partially done with the intention to damage the trade of Rhodes, which at the time was an enemy of Rome. In 167 or 166 BC, after the Romans won the Third Macedonian War, the Roman Republic ceded the island to the Athenians, who expelled most of the original inhabitants. Roman traders came to purchase tens of thousands of slaves captured by the Cilician pirates or in the wars following the disintegration of the Seleucid Empire, part of the former empire of Alexander the Great. Delos became thus the centre of the slave trade, having the largest slave market in the larger region. The destruction of Corinth by the Romans in 146 BC gave Delos the opportunity to at least partially supplant Corinth as the major commercial centre of Greece.

However, Delos's commercial prosperity, construction activity, and population diminished significantly after the island was destroyed by the forces of Mithridates VI, King of Pontus in 88 and 69 BC, during the Mithridatic Wars with Rome, since Delos was Rome's ally. By the end of the 1st century BC, trade routes had changed; Delos was no longer the centre of Italian trade with the East, and it also declined as a religious centre. Due to its inadequate natural sources, unlike other Greek islands, Delos did not have an indigenous, self-supporting community of its own. Consequently, in later times it was uninhabited.

Since 1873 the French School at Athens has been excavating the island, whose complex of buildings is on a par with those of Delphi and Olympia. In 1990, UNESCO inscribed Delos on the World Heritage List, citing it as an 'exceptionally extensive and rich' archaeological site which 'conveys the image of a great cosmopolitan Mediterranean port'.

Landmarks

The small Sacred Lake in its circular bowl, now intentionally left dry for hygienic reasons, is a topographical feature that determined the placement of the rest.

There are several markets. Among these, the Hellenistic agora of the Competaliasts by the Sacred Harbour retains the postholes for market shelters in its stone paving. Two powerful Italic merchant guilds dedicated statues and columns there.

The Doric temple of the Delians was dedicated to Apollo. Beside the temple once stood a colossal statue of this god, dating from the 6th century BC. Parts of the upper torso and pelvis remain in situ, a hand is kept at the local museum and a foot in the British Museum.

The 'Terrace of the Lions' was also dedicated to Apollo by the people of Naxos in the end of the 7th century BC. It originally had nine to twelve squatting, snarling marble guardian lions along the Sacred Way. The lions create a monumental avenue reminding of the Egyptian avenues of sphinxes. Today, seven of the original lions remain and one is inserted over the main gate to the Arsenal of Venice..

The House of the Naxians, dating from the first quarter of the 6th century BC, was a long hall with one central ionic colonnade.

The establishment of the Poseidoniasts, clubhouse of 'the Koinon of the Berytian Poseidoniast merchants, shipmasters and warehousemen', built in the early years of Roman domination, i.e. the late 2nd century BC.

The marble theatre is a rebuilding of an older one, which was dating from the beginning of the 3rd century BC.

The Doric temple of Isis was built on a high overlooking hill at the beginning of the Roman period to venerate the trinity of Isis, the Alexandrian Serapes and Anubis.

The temple of Hera, dating from around 500 BC, is a rebuilding of an earlier Heraion.

The House of Dionysus is a luxurious 2nd century BC private house named after the floor mosaic of Dionysus riding a panther. The House of Dolphins is similarly named after its atrium mosaic, where erotes ride dolphins. Many other luxurious dwellings are preserved and accessible to visitors.

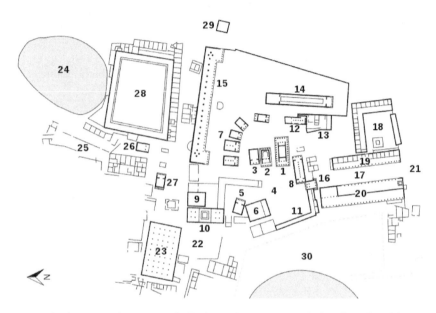

Plan of the sacred area of Delos. Source: Tomisti, CC BY-SA 4.0 <https://creativecommons.org/licenses/by-sa/4.0>, via Wikimedia Commons

1. Delian temple of Apollo
2. Athenian temple of Apollo
3. Poros temple of Apollo
4. Colossus of the Naxians
5. Temple of Artemis
6. Keraton
7. Treasuries
8. House of the Naxians
9. Ekklesiasterion
10. Thesmophoreion
11. Stoa of the Naxians
12. Bouleuterion
13. Prytaneion
14. Neorion or Bull Monument
15. Stoa of Antigonus
16. Propylon
17. Sacred Road
18. Agora of the Delians
19. South Stoa
20. Stoa of Philippus
21. Agora of the Competaliasts
22. Agora of Theophrastus
23. Hypostyle Hall or Stoa of Poseidon
24. Sacred Lake
25. Lion Terrace
26. Temple of Leto
27. Temple of Twelve Gods
28. Agora of Italians
29. Sanctuary of Dionysus or Stoibadeion
30. Sacred Harbour

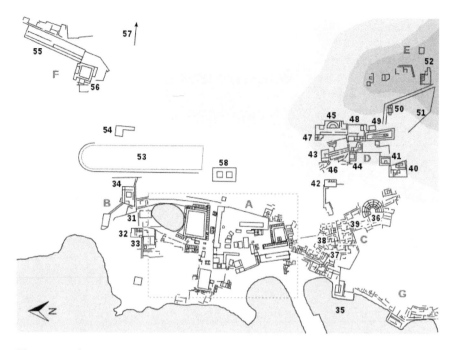

Plan of Delos. Source: Tomisti, CC BY-SA 4.0 <https://creativecommons.org/licenses/by-sa/4.0>, via Wikimedia Commons

Areas:

A. Area of the sanctuaries of Apollo and Artemis

B. Area of the Sacred Lake

C. Area of the theatre

D. Slope of the Mount Cynthus (Kynthos)

E. Mount Cynthus (Kynthos)

F. Area of the stadium

G. Harbours

Buildings (numbering continues from previous plan)

31. House of the Lake
32. House of Diadumenos
33. House of Poseidoniasts
34. Granite Palaestra
35. Trading Harbour
36. Theatre
37. House of Kleopatra
38. House of Dionysus

63

39. House of the Trident
40. House of Masks
41. House of Dolphins
42. House of Hermes
43. House of Inopos
44. Samothrakeion and Memorial of Mithridates
45. Sanctuary of Syrian Gods
46. Serapeion A
47. Serapeion B
48. Serapeion C, including temple of the Egyptians Gods and temple of Isis
49. Temple of Hera
50. Sanctuary of Agathe Tyche or Philadelpheion
51. Cave of Cynthus (Kynthos)
52. Cynthian Sanctuary of Zeus and Athena
53. Hippodrome
54. Archegesion
55. Stadium
56. Gymnasium
57. Synagogue
58. (Archaeological Museum)

A view from the ship reaching Delos from Mykonos

Above, one of the sculptures of Antony Gormley, exposed in the archaeological site at the time our group visited the island. Below, area of the sanctuaries

Area of the sanctuaries

Area of the sanctuaries

Above, area of the sanctuaries. Below, Terrace of the Lions

Above, the house of Hermes. Below, the house of Inopos

Above, the temple of Isis. Below, the view from the hill of Kynthos. On the left part of the photo, the house of Masks (the covered one on the left) and the house of Dolphins (right)

The view from the hill of Kynthos

Above, the house of Masks. Below, the theatre

Above, the house of the Trident. Below, the house of Kleopatra

The house of Dionysus

4 NAXOS. FROM THE PRECURSOR OF THE PARTHENON TO THE CRUSADERS

Naxos becomes the seat of the crusaders

Wondering how Greece was under the domination of the crusaders? It seems to be something lost in the oblivion of the past and we will never get any idea of how it was? Perhaps you haven't been in the right place. In Naxos, the less known part of Greek history exists and is alive like nowhere else.

During our hiking tour in Naxos, always under the guidance of Kostas, we found ourselves in the Castle of Chora (the capital). It's one of the best-preserved castles of the Aegean. And one of the few inhabited until today. This further increases its value. Which, anyway, is particularly great. Because this small piece of Naxos encapsulates a disproportionately important history.

In 1207, three years after the crusaders of the Fourth Crusade conquered the Byzantine Empire, Marco Sanudo, a Venetian nobleman, the nephew of the doge Enrico Dandolo, occupied most of the islands of the Cyclades. He founded the Duchy of the Archipelago and settled in Naxos.

A castle that stands out

Most medieval settlements of the Aegean have a makeshift fortification. Namely, the inhabitants built their houses close to each other, leaving the exterior walls blind. So they formed a wall that protected them from the greatest scourge of the Aegean for centuries: the pirates.

But Naxos was not a random settlement. It was the seat of the Duke. Here lived the leader of the Cyclades and the Venetian noblemen who accompanied him to the conquest of the islands. Therefore, here security requirements were greater. So they built a regular wall, with five towers at the corners. Today, only one is preserved, the tower of Glezos.

Inside, in the centre, they built the two centres of power, as in all medieval cities of Western Europe: the centre of political power, namely, the palace of the Duke; and the centre of religious authority, namely, the catholic cathedral. Should enemies manage to get inside the walls, there was also the last refuge: the defensive tower. There the inhabitants would give the battle to the end. Today it's in ruins, but it's still impressive.

About the palace of Sanudo scholars disagree. Others say it's the half-ruined defensive tower. Others that it was a separate building, the one now housing the Catholic Archdiocese.

The tower of Glezos, the only one of the five towers of the Castle still preserved

The defensive tower. Last resort if the enemies came through the walls

The Catholic Archdiocese. They say it was once the palace of Marco Sanudo

The Castle entrance from Pradouna Square

The Castle had three gates. We walked in through the most important, the Great Door (Trani Porta). On the pilaster, we saw engraved the Venetian cubit. When the draper came, the noblewomen of the Castle came to meet him at the Great Door. Thus, they used the engraved cubit to measure the fabrics they bought.

The Great Door (Trani Porta)

At the Metropolis of all Aegean

First, we entered the church of Candlemas. It's the Catholic cathedral of Naxos and seat of the Archbishop of Naxos and Tinos. He holds also the title of Metropolitan of all Aegean. The title is not random and reflects the island's history and the importance it had throughout the Aegean in the Middle Ages. Sanudo built the cathedral in the 13th century, but its present form dates from the 17th century.

The Catholic cathedral of Candlemas

In the centre of the sanctuary, there is the icon of the Virgin of Mercy. It's one of the oldest in Greece and perhaps the only one that presents the full-length Virgin Mary holding Jesus Christ. Archaeologists date it back to the 11th-12th century. It's two-sided and on the back side, there is an image of John the Baptist. The icon has always been in that place but covered by a newer layer and with silver on top, to the feet of Jesus Christ. Thanks to the insistence of the then vicar, Father Emmanuel Remoundos, and the teamwork of conservators from the Byzantine Museum of Athens the old icon was discovered in 1970. They placed it in a rotating frame so that also the back image could be visible.

The top of the steeple of the Catholic cathedral is the highest point in Naxos Town

Catholic cathedral of Candlemas. The Virgin of Mercy, one of the oldest icons in Greece

Afterwards, it was the turn of the Cappella Casazza, dedicated to the Immaculate Conception. They say it was the palace chapel of Sanudo. What is certain is that later it was the church of the Jesuit monastery. It's there that Father Emmanuel Remoundos, now former vicar, guides us. He tells us that the chapel is adjacent to the former Jesuit monastery, with which it communicates internally. He also reveals to us that it sits on the edge of the Castle, so its external side is in the air. Actually, the floor we step on has a huge gap underneath. He even shows us a drawing he made himself. It looks like a miniature of Mont Saint Michel in Normandy. What we think is the ground floor, is actually several floors above the ground.

Of course, we couldn't see this from within. But what we could see was a richly decorated baroque pulpit and respective altars with paintings of rare artistic value. And, as Father Emmanuel demonstrates to us, this space has excellent acoustics. Also, another rare element is the Gothic cross vault with ribs above the sanctuary. In other countries these things are common, but in Greece, they are very rare.

Next to the building of the Catholic Archdiocese, we visited the Virgin Mary Theoskepasti (Covered by God), the only Orthodox church in the Castle. Some say that it was already there when the Venetians arrived. Others, that Sanudo built it for his wife, who was Orthodox.

Cappella Casazza

Schools of international fame

The huge complex of the convent of the Ursulines

The most impressive building in the Castle, however, is the convent of the Ursulines, which housed one of the most famous schools in the Eastern Mediterranean. Three schools operated in the Castle in respective monasteries. A girls' school in the convent of the Ursulines and two for boys. One in the monastery of the Capuchins and one in that of the Jesuits.

The school of the Jesuits was later turned into a commercial school, under the order of the Salesians. Nikos Kazantzakis, the famous Greek author, studied here and became a great lover of Naxos.

One would expect that these monasteries were founded under the Venetians. And yet not. They were founded during the Ottoman domination. The Venetians were always in a great rivalry with the Pope and didn't approve the strengthening of the Catholic Church in their territories. Therefore, they didn't allow the establishment of Catholic monasteries. But when the Cyclades became finally Ottoman, in 1566, their Catholic population was a good excuse for French kings to intervene in the Ottoman Empire.

The convent of the Ursulines from the side of Aghia Kyriaki church, the favourite of the artists

King Francis had already signed in 1535 a treaty with Sultan Suleiman the Magnificent. According to it, all Catholics of the empire would be under his protection. The French kings sent French monks and nuns, who established monasteries in many islands. Later, when France changed policy, the French were replaced by locals. They keep these institutions until today.

Saint Anthony of Padua, the church of the monastery of the Capuchins

Some of them housed schools, which later became so famous for the good French education they offered, that they attracted pupils from as far as Madagascar. But initially, they were the first schools in these islands since ancient times. Perhaps King Francis hadn't the most altruistic motives, but we must admit that he offered a great service to the Cyclades and beyond.

The kitchen of the convent of the Ursulines

The Naxos convent of the Ursulines was founded in 1670 by local women of the Castle. Later, they were joined by French nuns. It was the first school for girls founded not only in Greece but throughout the Eastern Mediterranean! It operated for exactly 300 years, until 1970.

These schools fell, unfortunately, victims to the massive displacement of the inhabitants to Athens after World War II. The Ursulines, however, continue their educational tradition at the new schools that were established in the capital. Today, the building complex in Naxos houses the cultural centre 'Saint Ursula'.

The cultural centre 'Saint Ursula'

Museums in the Castle

Inside the Castle, we also saw the Archaeological Museum, housed in the former Jesuit monastery. Apart from the other very important exhibits, the collection of Cycladic figurines is the second largest after that of the National Archaeological Museum of Athens. Naxos occupied a prominent position in Prehistory, thanks to its size and central location in the Aegean Sea. The islands of the Aegean acted as a bridge uniting Europe to Asia and profited from the commercial activities between these lands, their ports receiving the ships which ensured that trade. The 3rd millennium BC, i.e. the Early Bronze Age, was the era of the so-called Cycladic civilization, which created these astonishing figurines. These works of art in local white marble impress by their abstract forms, which inspired many modern artists. At that time, Naxos had a dense population, installed in small settlements along the island's coast.

The courtyard of the Archaeological Museum (former Jesuit monastery)

However, the settlements of the Cycladic civilization had a violent end, which resulted in the interruption of this artistic creation. Around 2000 BC, the Cyclades started being influenced by the Minoan civilization of Crete, the new emerging power in the Aegean Sea. That led to a new period of prosperity in the Cyclades, which ended with the decline of Crete around 1500 BC and the arrival of the Mycenaeans, who dominated the last phase of Bronze Age in Greece.

Cydadic figurines in the Archaeological Museum of Naxos. Photo by Zde / CC BY-SA (https://creativecommons.org/licenses/by-sa/3.0)

Another museum we visited was the Venetian Museum, in the Dellarocca-Barozzi mansion. It has very interesting furniture and objects that give a lot of information about the history of Naxos. But the Dellarocca-Barozzi is not the only Venetian mansion. Walking in the Castle we saw many others that still preserve their escutcheons. Since the Castle buildings have retained their use (residential and religious buildings), the medieval fortified city seems to have remained untouched by time. Walking through the winding streets, you think the Duke of the Archipelago will appear around some corner.

Around the Castle

Saint Anthony. A typical Cycladic church from outside, Gothic inside. At the entrance, the cross of the Knights Hospitaller

Outside the Castle, you can complete your visit with two other monuments of Venetian times. One is the church of Saint Anthony the Hermit, in the harbour. From the outside, it looks like a typical Cycladic church. But inside it's Gothic. It was built around 1440 and later given to the Knights of Rhodes (Knights Hospitaller). That's why we see their characteristic cross at the entrance.

The other Venetian monument is the small church of the Virgin Mary of the Snow, in the market. Its strange name is linked to a tradition of Rome. On the night of August 4th to August 5th 356, the Virgin Mary appeared in a dream to a Roman nobleman named John and asked him to build a basilica at the place where it would have snowed in the morning.

Pope Liberius had the same dream. After having found out that it had actually snowed on one of the seven hills of Rome, the Esquilin, he ordered the construction of a church in honour of the Virgin Mary. They named the church Santa Maria ad Nives, namely, the Virgin Mary of the Snow. Later they built there one of the largest churches in the world and one of the most important monuments of Rome: Santa Maria Maggiore. The church of Naxos, of course, is just a Cycladic chapel. At first sight, however, because if you notice carefully you will see various details that again reveal the island's unique past.

A unique museum

Before leaving Chora, we visited the Site Museum, opposite the Orthodox cathedral of Zoodochos Pighi (Source of Life, built in 1787). It is a museum unique in Greece and one of very few of its kind in the whole world. Here, the exhibits are the findings which have been kept in the excavation site. They date from two periods: first, from the Mycenaean period (1300-1100 BC). After the decline of the Minoan civilization of Crete, which had greatly influenced the Cyclades, the islands played the role of a bridge for the expansion of the Mycenaean civilization, which had the city of Mycenae in the Peloponnese as its centre and dominated Greece at that time. An important settlement was then created in today's quarter of Grotta, where this museum is situated. From that period we can see a part of the city's walls and little pottery workshops, including non-baked pots placed on tables, basins once containing paints for the pots and a pottery kiln.

The Geometric period (900-700 BC) followed the two centuries of chaos engendered by the arrival of the Dorians in about 1100 BC and the subsequent fall of the Mycenaean civilization. Naxos is now mainly inhabited by Ionians who came from Attica and occupies once again a prominent position among the Greek powers. At that time, the use of this place changed and it became a sanctuary. A tumulus was created, which covered the tombs of prominent Naxians. We can still see an offering table with broken pottery around it.

After visiting Chora, we continued our routes in the inland of Naxos, which is a separate world, of an incredible monumental wealth.

The kouroi

I first got to know the hinterland of Naxos by road touring, with the local friend Nikos Gavalas, a member of our hiking group. A few years later, I had the opportunity to discover it by hiking, always under the guidance of Kostas.

So, after the castle of Naxos, now it's the turn of our hiking tour in one of the most monumental hinterlands of the Aegean. First, we will see the antiquities. From all the Cycladic islands, Naxos is the most suitable place to discover archaic Greece, which has prepared the classical world.

In the Archaic period (7th – 6th century BC), which followed the Geometric period, Naxos kept its already established prominent position and became a major naval power. Its economic progress was accompanied by a spectacular prosperity of the arts, and especially sculpture. The existence of marble in the island facilitated this development. The Naxians offered spectacular sculptures in the sanctuaries of Apollo in Delphi and Delos. The god's colossal statue and the famous lions in the Avenue of the Lions in the latter were offered by them. Delos, one of the most important sanctuaries of Greek Antiquity, became a dependence of Naxos, a fact demonstrating the island's importance. The rise of Athens in the 5th century BC marked the end of Naxos's preponderance, since Athens superseded it as the dominant power in the Cyclades. The political decline brought also the loss of its role in the evolution of Greek art.

The top artefacts of archaic sculpture are the kouroi and korai. In Naxos, there are not one, not two, but three kouroi of colossal dimensions. All three are abandoned unfinished in their quarries. It's unknown why they were not completed. Perhaps they are related to the seizure of the orders of wealthy citizens realised by the tyrant Lygdamis as soon as he took over.

Two of them, dating from the 7th century BC, are in Flerio. One in the olive grove of Evdokia Kondyli, who is an attraction herself with her narratives. In her cafe, in the olive grove, she will proudly narrate to you the discovery of the 'Greek' by her grandfather. She will also show you that even foreign guidebooks report her family as a guardian of the kouros, as its size doesn't allow its transfer to a museum. A similar case is the second kouros of Flerio. This one lies higher and is accessible only by hiking, which we, of course, did.

Above, the kouros in the olive grove of the Kondylis family. Below, the second kouros of Flerio. They both date from the 7th century BC. At the trail Myli - Flerio - Pano Potamia - Mesi Potamia - Kato Potamia

The most impressive, however, is the 6th-century BC kouros near the village of Apollonas. With a length of more than 10 meters, it's the largest. It's also the most 'advanced'. Some features and the beard can be distinguished. Some say it's Dionysus and others say it's Apollo. Some adventurous members of our group climbed up the steep rocks and took 'aerial' photos of it.

The kouros of Apollonas, more than 10 metres long, dating from the 6th century BC

The Parthenon was prepared in Naxos

But it's not just the kouroi. Naxos also has two sanctuaries - among many - of unique archaeological value. One is the sanctuary of Dionysus in Yria. The worship from the 14th to the 8th century BC was outdoors. Four consecutive buildings followed. The restored ruins we see belong to the last temple, of 580 BC (Archaic era). The temples of Yria are of huge archaeological importance, as they document with unique completeness the birth of the marble insular Greek architecture.

The other great sanctuary is in Gyroulas, near Sangri. Worship began in the 8th century BC and it was also originally outdoors. At the end of the 6th century BC, though, a monumental all-marble temple was built. The sanctuary, according to various indications, was dedicated to Apollo, Demeter and Kore, with an emphasis on their chthonic qualities.

The restored marble temple represents one of the most important steps in the evolution of Greek architecture. Since it's the oldest building where curves were observed, and also the first with marble tiles, it's no exaggeration to say that the Parthenon was prepared here. It's worth visiting not only the temple but also the exemplary museum. It should be noted that the restoration was awarded by the organisation Europa Nostra.

But there are also other archaeological finds. One of the most important is the aqueduct in Melanes. The area of Melanes has plenty of water. That's why the tyrant Lygdamis built an 11-km aqueduct that supplied the ancient city with water.

Yria, sanctuary of Dionysus, dating from 580 BC

Gyroulas, the restored sanctuary of Apollo, Demeter and Kore, dating from the end of the 6th century BC

Middle Ages. Naxos closes itself to its interior

After the Archaic period, Naxos lost its significance. Much later, however, in the first Byzantine centuries, monuments of unique value are again created.

The centuries from the 7th to the 9th are called the Dark Ages of Byzantium. After the glorious era of Justinian in the 6th century, the 7th century will see the appearance of the Arabs. The Arab pirates ravaging the coasts force the population, for the first time in Greek history, to withdraw to the hinterland. This is the first time Greece's population centre of gravity shifts from the coast to the interior. As was only natural, attacks by Arab pirates cause great turmoil and lead to a regression of civilisation.

As if that wasn't enough, in the next two centuries Byzantium is shaken by Iconomachy, the prohibition of religious images. It's a real civil war, which will lead to huge disasters of cultural heritage and not only. As a result of disasters and social unrest, from these three centuries, we have the least information, but also the least monuments and works of art. But Naxos is a strange and unexplained exception to this rule.

Right from this period, Naxos has a great number of monuments that make it again unique throughout Greece. Here is the largest ensemble of churches of Iconomachy. Along with them, an additional great number of Byzantine churches from other periods, which justly gave to Naxos the title of the 'Mystras of the Aegean'.

The majority of these monuments are located on the plateau of Tragaia. Tragaia constitutes the heart of Naxos and almost the entire population gathered here during the 'Dark Ages', to the security of the inland, as far as possible from the dangerous shores. Here you see only a small part of this wealth that we managed to visit in the limited for Naxos time of the six days we had.

As you will notice, the churches of Naxos have a rough structure and no exterior decoration. They are typical monuments of a self-sufficient rural society. That society managed, in times of great shortage of resources in the small Aegean islands, to create its own monuments by the means it had.

Chalki. Aghios Georgios (Saint George) Diasoritis, 11th century

Kerami. Saint John, 13th century

Metochi, near Monitsia. Holy Apostles, 10th-11th century. The only two-storey church in Naxos. At the trail Kaloxylos - Kerami - Akadimi Chalki

Rachi. Panaghia (Virgin Mary) Rachidiotissa, 12th-14th century. At the trail Chalki - Panaghia Drosiani

Monitsia. Saint Isidore, 6th-7th century. At the trail Chalki - Panaghia Drosiani. The first school of the Capuchins outside Chora was founded in Monitsia

Monastery of Kaloritsa, near Sangri, 11th-13th century, built over a cave converted into a church in the 4th century. Accessible via a trail from Bazaios tower

Panaghia (Virgin Mary) Drosiani. The crown of Naxian churches

The most important of the churches of Naxos is definitely Panaghia Drosiani, in the village of Moni. It dates back to the 6th century, while its frescoes date from the same century and the next. These make it an extremely rare monument. Besides, it has a very special architecture, which arose from additions of different times. You can reach it by hiking from Chalki and passing through many important Byzantine monuments of Tragaia.

With a rough structure and no exterior decoration, Panaghia Drosiani is a typical example of a Naxian church. Its strange shape is the result of additions dating from different times

Fotodotis (Giver of Light). A monastery built like a castle

The oldest monastery in Naxos is the impressive castle - monastery of Christ Fotodotis, which is considered to date from the 6th century. There are many legends and traditions about the monastery's foundation. Most prevalent is the one according to which the monastery was built by a princess. She was endangered by great seas and made a vow to build a church in the land where she would be saved. According to the same tradition, the princess saw some light at this point and, in keeping with her vow, built the monastery dedicated to the 'Giver of Light'.

The tripartite sanctuary betrays that it's not a simple castle. The monastery can be accessed via a trail from Aghia Marina

The most important iconoclastic church in Greece

As for the interior, however, the most impressive church in Naxos is Aghia Kyriaki. We approached it by hiking from Apiranthos. In complete contrast to its simple and humble outside, its interior decoration is something unique.

This is the most important iconoclastic decoration in Greece. An immense variety of shapes and colours compensates for the prohibition to represent sacred persons. Among them are the birds wearing scarves around their necks (!), for which there is no unanimous interpretation. Unfortunately, the publication of photos of this decoration is not allowed by the competent Ephorate of Antiquities.

In the traces of the crusaders. Naxos after 1204

In 1207, when Naxos is conquered by the crusaders after the fall of the Byzantine Empire, in 1204, the island is divided among several Venetian aristocrats who establish the feudal system of Western Europe. Every nobleman exploits a part of the island. In this, he builds his tower where he resides in order to control the exploitation of his lands.

Even after the formal incorporation of Naxos into the Ottoman Empire, in 1566, with the death of the last Duke, the feudal system survived until 1830, with the foundation of the Greek State. The difference after 1566 was that in some cases Greek rulers replaced the Venetians and took the Venetian towers or built their own.

Despite the toughness of the Venetian administration, the naval power of Venice reduced insecurity due to piracy. So the population and also the settlements grew. That's why, as in the other Cyclades, the old settlements present today mainly the form they took during the Venetian occupation.

The Fragopoulos - Dellarocca tower in Kourounochori. In the background, Melanes. In the centre of the tower's façade is the murder hole. From here, they poured boiling water on the invaders

Apiranthos. A Cretan touch in the heart of the Cyclades

Our routes could not leave Apiranthos out of the way. A special village, both for its beauty and for its cultural specificity. The local dialect suggests that the village was inhabited by Cretans, who must have arrived here as refugees. And as if that was not enough, there are five museums to see here!

Apiranthos. Saint Anthony

Hiking from Apiranthos to the emery mines and Moutsouna. Because Naxos also has mineral wealth. Emery was loaded at the port of Moutsouna

Kokkos tower, 17th century. At the trail Myli - Flerio - Pano Potamia - Mesi Potamia - Kato Potamia

Kaloxylos - Kerami - Akadimi - Chalki. Hiking through the villages of Tragaia

This hiking route is ideal for exploring the villages of Tragaia.

Kaloxylos

Akadimi. Markopolitis tower, 18th century

Chalki. The noble capital of Tragaia

Our hiking route in the Tragaia plateau brings us to Chalki. Capital of the island before the arrival of the Venetians, Chalki has always been the centre of the rich plateau of Tragaia.

In Chalki we participated in a guided tour of the Vallindras distillery, which since 1896 makes the famous citrus liqueur. As they explained to us, the citrus is made from leaves and not from fruit, as one would expect, judging from other liqueurs.

The position of Chalki as the 'capital' of Tragaia is demonstrated by the functions it houses. In the central square, there is even a gallery. More precisely, the photographer's Dimitris Gavalas gallery. From what he said to us, the animation of Chalki supports the presence of the gallery here, instead of Chora, for example, as anyone who doesn't know would think.

Approaching Chalki on foot. Tower of Barozzi - Grazia - Fragopoulos (17th century)

Chalki. The next image we see: Virgin Mary the Protothronos. Iconoclastic church of the 9th century. Inside, it has a synthronon (embedded stalls), rare feature in churches after the Early Christian period (4th-6th century)

Chalki. Above, the square. Below, the scarcity of space in the fortified medieval settlements made such interventions in the buildings' angles necessary, in order to permit the passage of loaded mules. The rather Arab decorative motive could be an import of Naxian seamen

Leaving Tragaia

Bazaios tower. It was built in 1600 as a monastery of the Holy Cross and functioned until the early 19th century

Aghia tower, 17th century

Filoti. Barozzi tower, 17th century

Jesuit resort. The abandoned monument

Hiking from the village of Melanes, we reached the Jesuit resort at Kalamitsia. It's a huge complex, built in the 17th century. It served as the resting place of the Jesuit missionaries who were running through the countryside of Naxos. Today, unfortunately, it remains unused and abandoned to its fate.

Portara. Transition to another dimension

And now a reversal in the chronological order of the monuments.

Since we left in the afternoon, when the sun began to set, the ideal setting to say goodbye to Naxos was Portara. Portara is on the small island of Palatia, united with Naxos. According to mythology, Theseus left Ariadne here on the way from Crete to Athens. Here Dionysus found her and married her. Here, they said, the first Dionysian Mysteries (feast in honour of Dionysus) took place.

Portara is a remnant of the incomplete colossal temple of Apollo. The tyrant Lygdamis attempted to build it in the 6th century BC, the age of the peak of ancient Naxos. Here you can see the island's most famous sunset. Here we 'walked through' the door leading out of Naxos. Not for long though. We renewed the appointment to try and discover more things from the countless ones that this island of unique cultural richness has.

Jesuit resort

Chora seen form the island of Palatia, where we went to see one of the most famous sunsets in Greece

Portara, a remnant of the incomplete colossal temple of Apollo (6th century BC) on the islet of Palatia

5 PAROS – ANTIPAROS – DESPOTIKO. THE BIRTHPLACE OF MARBLE MASTERPIECES

Paros. A jewel of ancient Greece

Paros, Antiparos and Despotiko form a complex in the very middle of the Cyclades, forming an ideal combination for the visitor who would like to combine fine beaches, an extraordinary landscape and a rich cultural heritage.

The Cyclades occupied a prominent position in Prehistory, thanks to their central location in the Aegean Sea. The islands of the Aegean acted as a bridge uniting Europe to Asia and profited from the commercial activities between these lands, their ports receiving the ships which ensured that trade. The 3rd millennium BC, i.e. the Early Bronze Age, was the era of the so-called Cycladic civilization, which created the world-famous astonishing Cycladic figurines. These works of art in local white marble impress by their abstract forms, which inspired many modern artists. At that time the Cyclades had a dense population, installed in small settlements along the islands' coasts and Paros experienced a particular prosperity.

However, the settlements of the Cycladic civilization had a violent end, which resulted in the interruption of this artistic creation. Around 2000 BC, the Cyclades started being influenced by the Minoan civilization of Crete, the new emerging power in the Aegean Sea. That led to a new period of prosperity in the Cyclades, which ended with the decline of Crete around 1500 BC and the arrival of the Mycenaeans, who dominated the last phase of Bronze Age in Greece (Mycenaean period, 1600-1100 BC).

The Geometric period (900-700 BC) followed the two centuries of chaos engendered by the arrival of the Dorians in about 1100 BC and the subsequent fall of the Mycenaean civilization. Paros is now mainly inhabited by Ionians who came from Attica.

In the Archaic period (7th – 6th century BC), which followed the Geometric period, the Cyclades experienced a new era of prosperity. Paros established colonies in Thasos and Parium on the Hellespont. In the former colony, which was founded in 680 BC, the lyric poet Archilochus, one of the most important ancient Greek poets and a native of Paros, is said to have taken part. In 385 BC the Parians, along with Dionysius of Syracuse, founded a colony on the Illyrian island of Pharos (Hvar in Croatia).

However, in the Classical period all the Cyclades declined with the rise of Athens in the 5th century BC and their compulsory adhesion to the Athenian Alliance, which transformed them into Athens's satellites. Paros paid the highest tribute of the island members: 30 talents annually, according to the estimate of Olympiodorus (429 BC). This implies that Paros was one of the wealthiest islands in the Aegean.

Paros marble, which is white and translucent, with a coarse grain and a beautiful texture, was the chief source of wealth for the island. Its translucidity can reach 6-7 cm and sometimes even 30 cm, while the translucidity of the famous Carrara marble is of 2,5 cm. 70% of the sculptures in the areas surrounding the Aegean Sea have been made of Paros marble! The famous marble quarries lie on the northern side of the mountain formerly known as Marathi (afterwards Capresso).

The marble, whose exportation started in the 6th century BC, was used by many great Greek sculptors. Venus de Milo and Hermes of Praxiteles are some of the masterpieces made of it. It was obtained from subterranean quarries driven horizontally or at a descending angle into the rock. The marble thus extracted by lamplight was given the name of Lychnites, Lychneus (from lychnos, a lamp), or Lygdos. Several of these tunnels are still to be seen and form the largest artificial cave in Greece. At the entrance to one of them is a bas-relief dedicated to the god Pan and the nymphs.

Paros has also been homeland to various famous personalities of the Antiquity, such as the sculptor Agoracritus (5th century BC), the aforementioned lyric poet Archilochus (around 680 BC–around 645 BC), the sculptor and architect Scopas (around 395–350 BC) and the sculptor Thrasymedes (4th century BC). The island's school of sculpture was famous all over Greece.

Contrary to most of the Cyclades who declined during Roman domination, Paros continued being a considerable naval power with a thriving economy and an important cultural activity.

In 1204, the soldiers of the 4th crusade seized Constantinople and occupied the Byzantine Empire, dividing its territories among them. Paros became subject to the Duchy of the Archipelago, a fiefdom made up of most of the Cyclades and ruled by a Venetian duke, who had his capital in Naxos. The first duke and founder of this State was the Venetian nobleman Marco Sanudo, who occupied these islands on behalf of the Venetian Republic. This made the duchy a client State of the metropolis. In the end of the 14th century, however, Paros became the centre of a separate fiefdom, vassal of the Duchy of the Archipelago, most of the time ruled by the Sommaripa family.

In 1537, Paros was conquered by the Ottomans, although it officially remained under the authority of the Duke of the Archipelago, until the death of the last duke in 1566. Then, the islands forming the duchy were officially incorporated into the Ottoman Empire until the Greek Revolution of 1821. At this time, Paros became the home of a heroine of the nationalist movement, Manto Mavrogenous, who had both financed and fought in the Revolution. Her house is today a historical monument.

Parikia. The charm of an island capital

The capital of Paros, Parikia, situated on a bay on the north-west side of the island, occupies the site of the ancient capital Paros. Its present name dates from the early Byzantine times, when 'parikoi' (serfs) of the monastery of Ekatontapyliani settled here. In Parikia, houses are built and decorated in the traditional Cycladic style, with flat roofs, whitewashed walls and blue-painted doors and window frames and shutters. Shadowed by luxuriant vines, and surrounded by gardens of oranges and pomegranates, the houses give the town a particularly picturesque aspect.

Above the central stretch of the seafront road, stands the hill of Kastro (Castle), the oldest part of Parikia, at the site of the ancient town of Paros. It includes the remains of a medieval fortress, built by the Venetians almost entirely of the marble ruins of ancient temples dedicated to Athena, Apollo and Demeter. Similar traces of antiquity, in the shape of bas-reliefs, inscriptions, columns etc are numerous in the buildings of this medieval settlement.

In this part of the town dating from the time of Venetian domination, the locals built their houses attached to one another, for protection against pirates. Thus, they formed a continuous outer front, with no openings, like a fortification. The lack of space was such, that they even built parts of their houses above the streets.

Should enemies manage to get inside the walls, there was also the last refuge: the defensive tower. This is one of the most extraordinary monuments in Paros, since it is built entirely of ancient material. We can even distinguish the drums (rings) of ancient columns.

The church of Saint Constantine dominates the hill of the Castle, the oldest part of Parikia, at the site of the ancient town of Paros. The re-use of ancient material in it is obvious (below)

A characteristic street in the Castle of Parikia. The curve corresponds to the concentric rings of houses surrounding the dwelling of the Venetian rulers. The distance of each ring from this dwelling depended on the social rank of its inhabitants, the Venetian aristocracy residing closest to their chief

Castle of Parikia. Part of the medieval fortification walls, made of ancient materials

A drum of an ancient column is now a table for a house in the Castle of Parikia. The extensive use of ancient marble remains in modern constructions by the island's inhabitants is widely mentioned by European travellers during the Ottoman domination

The defensive tower in the middle of the Castle. Last resort if the enemies came through the walls. It is an astonishing structure, built entirely of ancient remains. We can even distinguish the drums (rings) of the columns of ancient temples

An elegant solution to the problem of extending the houses within the limited space of fortified medieval settlements

Yet another elegant solution to the scarcity of space in medieval settlements

Out of the medieval core of the Castle, we enter the part of Parikia built after Independence. In its main street, you will see a very different sight, diverging from the stereotypical image of a Cycladic settlement. Here, the houses are neoclassical. When Greece became an independent State in 1830, classicism was introduced by the Bavarian King Otto, a fervent admirer of ancient Greece and was supposed to form the link with the ancient past.

Therefore, public buildings were made according to this style and the upper classes who wanted to be 'modern' and 'European' adopted it with enthusiasm in their mansions. However, the people remained attached to traditional architecture, which better served their daily needs and was better adapted to the country's climate conditions and their financial means, adding neoclassical details occasionally so as not to be left out of the rebirth of ancient culture in its cradle, as classicism was seen at the time.

Since the Cyclades were islands of particularly restricted wealth, here neoclassical architecture was usually limited to public structures and very few houses of the most wealthy citizens. The exceptions were the islands of the ship-owners, Syros and Andros. The houses of Parikia's main street are a testimony of the existence of a wealthy class who had the means to build purely neoclassical dwellings.

One of the three fountains constructed in 1777 by Mavrogenis, the local great personality of the late Ottoman era, in front of the double church of the Holy Trinity and Saint Paraskevi (1626)

The neoclassical houses of Parikia's main street are a testimony of the existence of a prosperous class who had the means to build them, contrary to less wealthy inhabitants who remained attached to the less demanding traditional architecture

The presence of this carved marble frame in the door of a rather humble chapel is characteristic of the existence of marble and of the subsequent tradition on an island of very restricted means before the tourist era

Parikia, Panaghia Ekatontapyliani. Its purely Byzantine style contrasts with the Cycladic traditional architecture surrounding it

Parikia, Panaghia Ekatontapyliani. The baptistery with the cruciform font

Ekatontapyliani

Back from the port is the town's principal church, Panaghia Ekatontapyliani, literally meaning 'Virgin Mary of the hundred doors'. According to tradition, it has 99 apparent doors and one hidden one. This last one will be revealed when the Greeks will take again Constantinople. It is said to have been founded by the mother of the Roman Emperor Constantine the Great (306–337), Saint Helen, during her pilgrimage to the Holy Land. Its present form dates mainly from the time of Emperor Justinian (6th century AD). It is one of the most important Early Christian churches in Greece and certainly the island's supreme religious monument. There are two adjoining chapels, one of very early form, and also a baptistery with a cruciform font, the oldest and best preserved baptistery in the whole Orthodox East.

Next to Ekatontapyliani is the Catholic church of Saint Anthony and the adjacent monastery of the Capuchins, destroyed in 1770 by the men of the Russian fleet which had occupied the island in 1770-1774, during the conflict between Russia and the Ottoman Empire. The presence of a Catholic community is due, like in many other islands of the Cyclades, to the long Venetian domination.

Behind Ekatontapyliani is a zone of important archaeological findings, with ancient workshops of pottery and sculpture. Parikia has also a small but interesting archaeological museum housing some of the many findings from sites in Paros. Among them a fragment of the Parian Chronicle, a remarkable chronology of ancient Greece. Inscribed in marble, its entries give time elapsed between key events from about 1500 BC to 264 BC.

Lefkes

Lefkes (Poplars) is a particularly picturesque inland mountain village. It was founded in the 16th century and was the island's capital during the Ottoman domination (1566-1830), as it happened in many islands of the Aegean during the time of piracy, for safety reasons. Its first settlers came from Crete and the Peloponnese, but also from other settlements of the island by the seaside, in order to avoid pirates. Strolling through its winding streets is a particularly authentic experience in this highly touristy island.

Lefkes is connected to the village of Prodromos by the Byzantine Way, a trail dating from about one thousand years ago. It is covered with marble slabs and goes through a beautiful landscape of olive trees and vines.

Above: the church of the Holy Trinity in Lefkes, with its marble bell towers. Below: the scarcity of space in the fortified medieval settlements made such interventions in the buildings' angles necessary, in order to permit the passage of loaded mules. The rather Arab decorative motive could be an import by Parian seamen

A characteristic street of Lefkes

Photo by Denis Roubien

A total contrast to the previous photo: the popular version of classicism. Symmetry and classical decorative details add a majestic note to a building which, for the rest, is a traditional construction. The way of the poor to participate with their modest means in the vision of revival of the ancient past in reborn Greece after 1830

Naousa

On the north side of the island is the bay of Naousa, which provides a safe and spacious harbour. In ancient times it was closed by a chain. Although this fishing village (which acquired its present form in the 15th century) is extremely touristy, it is still very picturesque and certainly worth a visit. Its most important sight is the Venetian fortress (kastelli).

Naousa. Photo by Tango7174 / CC BY-SA
(https://creativecommons.org/licenses/by-sa/4.0)

Antiparos

Antiparos, the ancient Oliaros, has always been closely connected to Paros. Like Paros, it has been part of the Duchy of the Archipelago since 1207, but in 1440 it was taken through marriage by the Venetian family Loredan. Its ruler Leonardo Loredan built the castle of Antiparos, the island's most important architectural monument, one of the most impressive fortified settlements of the Aegean and very different from most of them. Most of the other similar settlements, like that of Parikia, were created in a random way by building the houses next to one another, thus creating irregular rings surrounding the central tower, last resort in case of attack and often also the ruler's dwelling. Here, the rows of houses surrounding the defensive tower (now destroyed) form a rectangular block, containing three-storey houses of the same size and form. Between this exterior block and the defensive tower are other, less regular blocks.

The island's other famous attraction is its cave, one of the most important of its kind, with stalactites and stalagmites. One of the latter is the oldest in Europe, 45 million years old.

Despotiko

This little island, the Prepesinthos of ancient times, lies southwest of Antiparos. It is uninhabited today, but it has been home to one of the greatest sanctuaries of ancient Greece, dedicated to Apollo, like the sanctuary of Delos, which finally overshadowed it. The ongoing extensive restoration works have already transformed the archaeological site, which is now extremely interesting and worth visiting.

6 SANTORINI. IN SEARCH OF THE AUTHENTIC

Firostefani. First view of the caldera

During our hikes, always under the direction of Kostas, we found ourselves in Santorini.

As our hotel was in Firostefani, one of the unified villages forming the agglomeration of the island's capital, at the edge of the caldera, we started with a walk along what is perhaps the most famous coast in Greece.

The Santorini caldera is a bay delimited by the different islands of the Santorini archipelago, consisting of a submerged caldera and surrounded by cliffs. This caldera was formed around 1600 BC during the volcanic eruption that caused the destruction of part of the ancient island, which already had a smaller caldera. Its remains are the present islands of Santorini, Thirassia and Aspronissi.

The caldera of Santorini, seen from Firostefani, one of the unified villages forming the agglomeration of the island's capital. The village that can be seen in the background is Imerovigli, the agglomeration's northern end. To the left of it, the rock of Skaros, where the island's medieval capital lay, now vanished

Views from the rooftops of Firostefani. In the background, the island of Thirassia. On the left, the island of Nea Kameni, created by the volcano

The last volcanic activity took place in 1950 AD. Parts of the Santorini volcano are the islands of Palia Kameni (Old Burnt, created in 46-47 AD) and Nea Kameni (New Burnt, created in 1707-1711 AD), the Kolumbo underwater volcano (active, created in 1650 AD) and the Christiana islands. Santorini belongs to the volcanic arc of the Aegean and is characterised as an active volcano along with Methana, Milos and Nisyros.

This church of Firostefani doesn't ring a bell, does it? And yet, its blue dome, not visible in this photo, is the archetypal image of Greece, appearing in the foreground of all the Santorini posters. On the other hand, its façade, much less typical, is unknown. It's the Catholic church of the Assumption of the Virgin Mary, known as Our Lady of Saints Theodores. It was named after the two small churches (of the Virgin Mary and Saints Theodores), also Catholic, whose place it took. The church was built to house an icon brought around 1570 by a local sailor. As it had come from Russia and was, therefore, of Byzantine style and made by an Orthodox painter, the island's Orthodox considered that it belonged to them and seized it several times, giving it back on every occasion only after the intervention of the Patriarch of Constantinople

The Catholic district. The Santorini of the crusaders

If you enter Fira, the capital proper, by Firostefani, like us, you will first go through the Catholic district, which occupies the highest site, according to the privileged social rank of its creators. These were the members of the Venetian nobility who ruled the island for centuries and part of the Greek nobility who adopted Catholicism to approach them.

In 1207, three years after the conquest of the Byzantine Empire by the crusaders of the Fourth Crusade, Marco Sanudo, a Venetian nobleman, the nephew of Doge Enrico Dandolo, occupied most of the Cyclades. He founded the Duchy of the Archipelago and settled in Naxos.

Santorini, like other islands, was divided between several Venetian aristocrats who established the feudal system of Western Europe. The Venetians built five citadels, for the protection of the population against pirates, who were wandering in the Aegean Sea, constituting a continual threat. These five citadels (called 'kastelli' - 'kastellia' in plural) were those of Skaros (the capital), Oia, Pyrgos, Emporio and Akrotiri.

Each nobleman exploited part of the island. There, he built his tower where he resided, in order to control the exploitation of his lands. This tower was fortified, to resist a possible pirate attack. In Santorini, this tower is called 'goulas'.

The Catholic district of Fira, seen from Firostefani. In the foreground, the church of Saint Stylianos. In the background, at a lower level, the rest of the island's capital

145

The monastery of the Lazarists, founded in 1783

It can be said that the Catholic district is the only part of Fira to have preserved much of its authenticity and therefore it deserves to be explored. The rest of the island's capital was completely rebuilt after the 1956 earthquake and therefore, unfortunately, lost its character.

The first monument we encountered on our way from Firostefani was the monastery of the Lazarists, founded in 1783, which housed a very famous school.

Then, the Catholic cathedral of Saint John the Baptist, dating from 1823. Santorini is the seat of a Catholic diocese, which demonstrates its importance at the time of Venetian domination. Religious power was then always combined with political power, which means that the seats of Catholic bishops were on the islands housing political leaders (for example, Naxos, formerly the seat of the Duke of the Archipelago, is still the seat of the Archbishop of Naxos, Primate of Greece, who also holds the title of Metropolitan of All Aegean).

Beside the cathedral are the convents of the Daughters of Charity and the Dominicans. The first, founded in 1841, housed a school and several charitable institutions. That of the Dominicans, the island's oldest convent; has the particularity of sheltering nuns of several nationalities. It was founded in 1596 in Skaros and transferred to Fira in 1811. The present complex was built between 1818 and 1862.

Above, the convents of the Daughters of Charity, dating from 1841 (left), and the Dominicans, founded in 1596 (in the background). Below, the Ghisi Palace, cultural centre of the Catholic Diocese of Santorini, dating from 1700

The Catholic cathedral of Saint John the Baptist, dating from 1823

Cruise in the caldera. The volcano

The next morning, we made the typical tourist cruise in the caldera and at the volcano, namely, the islands of Nea Kameni and Palia Kameni.

Island of Nea Kameni

Above, Oia, the most famous village of Santorini, seen from the sea, during the cruise in the caldera. Later on, we will reach it through the trail from Fira. Below, Fira, seen from the sea, during the cruise in the caldera

Thirassia. The authentic Santorini

But after the cruise, we started the most original part of our journey: a visit to Thirassia. This little island, still untouched by tourism, is the ideal place for those who want to see how Santorini was before the tourist flow that has transformed it forever.

The church of Saint Demetrius in the village of Potamos (River). The polychrome decoration of this bell tower, so different from the exclusive white and blue of the Aegean Sea (which, however, remains present) will probably remind you of Latin America

The first interesting sights that we saw were some churches with a polychrome decoration (exterior and interior) that reminded us of those of Latin America. As churches of this type are not found even in Santorini itself, their presence in this seemingly isolated island with little contact with the outside world is a mystery that remains to be elucidated.

Another polychrome decoration, on the façade this time. Saint Spyridon in the village of Potamos, dating from 1875

The scale of this church (Presentation of the Virgin Mary, dating from 1887) in the abandoned village of Agrilia (Wild Olive Tree) reveals that things have been very different for this island, today very scarcely inhabited. Below, a traditional oven seen from the same church

Agrilia. As we approach this church (Presentation of the Virgin Mary), huge for Thirassia, we see an even more polychrome façade, which has its counterpart in the decor of the interior. On the opposite page, the dwellings dug in the volcanic soil, such as one could once see in Santorini itself, before the tourist era. Here we can see how the Cycladic villages were at the time of piracy, when they were not whitewashed, so that they could not be seen. The use of lime outside was not imposed until the 1930s, for hygienic reasons

Above, the image presented by the village of Agrilia must not differ too much from the image of similar villages of Prehistoric Times. Below, on the trail leading from Manolas, the main village of Thirassia, to the island's southern tip. We can see the use of stones from the eruption as a building material

Continuing the hike from Manolas, the main village, to the island's southern tip. In the background, on both photos, we can distinguish Oia

The southern tip of Thirassia and, at the top, the monastery of the Dormition of the Virgin Mary or Panaghia Kera (The Virgin Our Lady). On the left, the volcano (Palia Kameni and Nea Kameni). Below, the view from the monastery towards the island's northern tip, seen in the background

Above, the monastery of the Dormition of the Virgin Mary. Below, the quintessence of Cydadic architecture: a stone and lime sculpture, glittering in the sun, between the sea and the sky

The wine festival. Another remnant of authenticity

This day is over in Finikia, a village very close to Oia, but very different. The difference is that, unlike its famous neighbour, this village seems very little affected by mass tourism. This is also corroborated by the wine festival taking place here.

It's the feast of Saint Matrona (October 20th), which lasts until morning, when they open the barrels of the year's new wine. We didn't have the courage to stay until morning, but we had the opportunity to participate in the only traditional 'panighyri' (religious festival accompanied by music and dance) surviving on the island, where one can still live the authentic atmosphere of the Cyclades of the past.

Finikia. An inverted pot serving as a chimney, usual in the Cyclades

Finikia. Above, a kanava, the place where Santorini's famous wine was or still is produced, transformed into a dwelling. It's the summer house of the chief of our group

From Fira to Oia. Hiking along a natural wonder

Nea Kameni

The next day, we started on the longest trail of our journey, from Fira to Firostefani, Imerovigli and Oia.

Above, Skaros, the island's medieval capital. The whole rock was covered with buildings in the Middle Ages. Below, Oia, at the northern tip of Santorini

Looking backwards, towards Fira. Skaros can be seen on the right, in the background

Oia. The captains' village

And, finally, we entered the famous Oia. In fact; it's famous for its sunset, which attracts an incredible number of visitors. But, aside from that, Oia has an impressive set of 'kapetanospita' (captains' houses). Oia, in the 19th century, was the third naval force in Greece, after the islands of Hydra and Spetses, largely contributing, like them, to the success of the Greek Revolution of 1821.

But, to see these houses, you must leave the touristy pedestrian zone along the caldera and wander in the alleys inside the village; what few tourists do, judging by the small number of them that we met.

As the visitor will notice, these houses don't have much to do with the rest of the village: they are neoclassical. When Greece became an independent State in 1830, classicism was introduced by the Bavarian King Otto, a fervent admirer of ancient Greece.

However, it was observed more faithfully by the upper class, who wanted to be 'modern' and 'European'. The people remained attached to traditional architecture, which better served their daily needs, adding neoclassical details occasionally so as not to be left out of the rebirth of ancient culture in its cradle, as classicism was seen at the time.

The houses of Oia follow, for the most part, a very specific type: a door in the middle, flanked by four windows and a semicircular window above it. The openings are separated from each other by pilasters.

The remains of the citadel of Oia, one of the five that existed in Santorini

One of the few really authentic parts of Oia along the caldera, since most of the village was rebuilt after the 1956 earthquake

A neoclassical house diverging from the type proper to Oia in the details (but not in essence). It belongs to the most classical type of all Greece and especially the capital (more elaborate details and of a superior quality of execution, from the stucco to the gate of the courtyard)

163

The fall of the plaster allows us to see the use of stones from the eruption as a building material

Mesaria. An impressive industrial heritage

The next day, we started with a visit to the village of Mesaria, completely ignored by tourists. It's a pity, because it has an impressive set of neoclassical houses worthy of Athens, centre of Greek classicism! This is explained by its industrial past (the famous wine and other products), which brought great wealth to its inhabitants, at a time when classicism was at its peak in Greece. This style was then the symbol of the upper bourgeoisie, which all the others imitated to the extent of their means, as we already saw with the captains' houses at Oia. But here, the means of the owners have allowed a reproduction of the same quality as the mansions of the country's capital.

Mesaria. Arghyros mansion, one of the island's most important wine producer families. It's the only one open to the public in all Santorini

Pyrgos. Lost in a medieval labyrinth

Our next stop was the fortified village of Pyrgos (Tower). Most of the medieval settlements of the Aegean Sea have fortuitous fortifications. Namely, the inhabitants built their houses close to each other, leaving the outer walls blind. They thus formed a wall that protected them from the greatest scourge of the Aegean for centuries: pirates.

On the other hand, the fortified settlements of Santorini seem to belong to those built in a seemingly fortuitous way, but in fact according to an organised and voluntarily complicated plan. They thus formed a labyrinth where the inhabitants could move easily but the pirates, in case they succeeded to enter, would be lost and trapped and, therefore, easily defeated. The citadel of Naxos, the capital of the Duchy of the Archipelago, belonged to this type and probably constituted the model for other settlements of the same category.

Pyrgos has a well-preserved 'kastelli' (walled settlement), which is one of the best examples of this type of inhabited complex, the other example being that of Emporio. The other three 'kastellia' are poorly preserved (we have already seen Skaros and Oia).

Above, around the citadel of Pyrgos, neoclassical houses clearly influenced by the captains' houses in Oia. Below, the entrance to the citadel (kastelli) of Pyrgos. The medieval settlement lies inside it and all that surrounds it is posterior, built after the creation of the Greek State in 1830, which marked the end of piracy in the Aegean Sea

The limited space resulting from their concentration inside the walls forced the inhabitants to find solutions to create room for everyone. Thus, the houses were extended over the street and created covered passageways.

photo by Denis Roubien

Into the citadel's labyrinth. One of the many covered passages, providing extra space from above. This was necessary in the confined space of a medieval settlement, where the houses were attached to one another in order to create a wall for protection against pirates. We arrive at a 'clearing', which turns out to be a churchyard

Thera. The ancient city

Next stop: ancient Thera. The celebrity of the prehistoric city of Akrotiri often makes forget that Santorini was also important in historic times. Its capital was Thera, which bears the island's ancient name, when it was colonised by the Spartans in the 8th century BC, after having remained uninhabited for centuries, since the eruption of the 17th century BC.

The city can be reached through stairs on the mountainside. In its present form, it has mainly remains of the Hellenistic and Roman era, since constant inhabitation didn't leave many traces from the first centuries of the city's existence.

The chapel of Saint Stephen, built with ancient materials in the 8th century AD: At that time, the Arab incursions forced the island's inhabitants to seek refuge in the ancient city in ruins, which they had abandoned in the 3rd century AD for the coast, which was safe then. The low construction quality reflects the decline in the standard of living compared to antiquity

View of Kamari, northeast of Thera. It was one of the ancient city's two ports

The agora (market)

Houses and workshops

View of Perissa, southeast of Thira, the ancient city's other port

An underground reservoir belonging to the sanctuary of Apollo Karneios

Vlychada. Another natural wonder

Our day ended at the beach of Vlychada, in Santorini's southern coast. Here we saw another natural wonder, which is unjustly much less famous than the caldera. On the other hand, this means that, even in summer, it's much less crowded and therefore pleasanter. Since it seems impossible to describe it, the reader is left to judge by the photos.

Emporio. the unknown architectural jewel

The next day started with a visit to Santorini's most interesting 'kastelli', Emporio. This fortified settlement started being created around 1450. Here, as in all the citadels of Santorini, just outside the entrance or a short distance from it, there was a church of Saint Theodosia, protector of fortifications.

The 'goulas' (defensive tower), lying out of the citadel, dates back to the 15th or 16th century. It must have been built when the citadel had already begun to form. The tower was probably used to store agricultural products and protect the farmers. It belonged to the D'Argenta family.

After the 17th century, when piracy declined, the tower became a dependence of the monastery of Saint John the Evangelist of Patmos (one of the most important of the Aegean, as it is believed that the Apocalypse was written there) and some of its monks lived in it.

The 'goulas' (defensive tower) of Emporio, out of the 'kastelli' (citadel)

The entrance to the most impressive citadel of Santorini. After entering it, we got lost in the most beautiful labyrinthine network of winding alleys

Also here, like in Pyrgos, we can see many covered passages, providing extra space from above, in the limited area of the fortified settlements of the Aegean

photo by Denis Roubien

photo by Denis Roubien

photo by Denis Roubien

photo by Denis Roubien

Akrotiri. The Greek Pompeii

This is what remains of the citadel (kastelli) of Akrotiri. In medieval times, Akrotiri was one of the island's citadels and was called La Ponta. In the centre of the settlement was the goulas (defensive tower), which suffered serious damage during the 1956 earthquake, although it had remained in a very good condition until then. In 1336, the Duke of the Archipelago Nikolaos Sanudo granted Akrotiri to the Gozzadini family, originally from Bologna. The fact that they were from this Italian city and not Venice, which was at war with the Ottoman Empire, associated with the citadel's defensive ability, allowed the Gozzadini family to retain possession even after the rest of Santorini was conquered by the Turks, in 1537. Finally, it passed to the Ottomans only in 1617

The visit of the island ended with its most unique and spectacular sight: the prehistoric city of Akrotiri (named after the neighbouring village), the Pompeii of Greece. It's a city buried by the eruption of the volcano at the end of the 17th century BC.

The excavated site that can be visited (14 acres) is just a portion of the prehistoric city, whose exact area is not known, since the excavations, started systematically only in 1967, continue.

Data on the occupation of Thera in Prehistory began to appear from the second half of the 19th century, when prehistoric antiquities were discovered in 1866 due to the use of volcanic earth by the French engineer Ferdinand de Lesseps, in order to insulate the walls of the Suez canal.

Professor Spyridon Marinatos began the excavations in Akrotiri in order to prove an old theory of his own, which he published in 1939 as ephore of the antiquities in Crete. According to this theory, the eruption of the Santorini volcano caused the collapse of the Minoan civilization of Crete.

The initial dating of the explosion was based on comparative studies of clay pottery and Egyptian sources, and it was estimated that the volcanic eruption that destroyed the city had taken place around the year 1500 BC. The absolute dating, however, made on the basis of radioactive carbon and dendrochronology shifted the date from 100 to 150 years earlier, while the most recent radioactive carbon dating of an olive branch buried by the ash of the explosion places the date between 1627 and 1600 BC, the interval between 1614 and 1613 BC being the most likely. The new dating proves the non-connection of the explosion with the destruction of the Minoan civilization, which happened much later, in the 15th century BC, and was more of a decadence.

It is believed that the so-called 'Minoan eruption' of Thera was even stronger than that of the Krakatoa volcano (Indonesia) in 1883. Because of the great power of the eruption that caused great geological changes on the island and the emergence of the volcanic cone of Nea Kameni (where the volcanic crater is today), but also because of the island's shape (it resembles a crescent), Thera was linked to the myth of the sunk Atlantis, as Plato described it.

About the time of the eruption, it is believed that it was spring, as pollen grains of olives and coniferous trees have been discovered in the layer of explosion materials.

According to the findings of the excavations, it is known that the area of Akrotiri was first inhabited around 4500 BC and had evolved to a city in the 18th century BC. At the beginning of the 17th century BC the earthquakes caused much damage, but many of the buildings were repaired and others remained unchanged, while new buildings were constructed near the old ones and the city was enlarged. The settlement flourished at the end of the Cycladic period until its burial by the 'Minoan eruption'. At the same time, the new palaces were in full swing in Minoan Crete.

The location was ideal for a safe harbour, as it was protected against north winds, while the soil morphology favoured the development of agriculture. It is thought that it was the island's capital, but this has not been confirmed yet.

The large number of frescoes in which many of the buildings' rooms are decorated, usually the upper floors, reveals a developed and sophisticated bourgeois society, which dressed with luxury, elegance and an impressive wealth of colours.

The fact that not a single human skeleton has been found in the city reveals that a number of warning earthquakes made the inhabitants leave on time. In any case, before the city was buried by the stones and ashes of the volcanic eruption, it was struck by a great earthquake, but it didn't stop being inhabited then.

However, other phenomena precursors of the volcanic explosion forced the inhabitants to leave the city, as evidenced by the fact that the works of clearing of the streets were never completed, while a large number of pots has been found on piles of rubble, where, apparently, they had been placed temporarily to be moved to safer places.

Also, indications of the state of emergency that prevailed in those days in the city, but also of the inhabitants' conviction that one day they would return to their homes, we gather from the clay vessels, the fabrics and the utensils of various materials found accumulated under doors or in niches of the rooms.

There is no evidence of where the inhabitants fled. The time, however, between the great earthquake and the eruption should not exceed a few weeks, while the time from the first explosions to the creation of the caldera is estimated at two to three days.

The successive waves of pumice and ash dragged the roofs and the upper parts of the settlement's buildings. After the eruption and the deposition of the volcanic materials that led to the city's burial, a torrential rain followed, which caused the erosion of pumice and ash and in many cases reached even the pre-eruption ground. This rain transferred fluid sludge to the buildings' ground floors, which led to the preservation of both their content and (in many cases) the floors of the overlying levels.

The urban fabric was dense and consisted of buildings of two or three floors and several rooms, organised warehouses, workshops, excellent urbanism with streets, squares and a drainage system.

The richest buildings were made of carved stones from volcanic rocks with a particularly rough surface. The rest of the buildings were made of irregular stones at their outer walls and straw-reinforced mud bricks, wood and plaster at the lighter inner walls of the upper floors. The foundations were generally shallow and there was often an artificial backfilling.

The pavements of the ground floor rooms were made of pressed soil or shale slabs, and in one case of broken shells (of the sea snails that gave the Tyrian red) and black pebbles, while those of the upper floors were made of wood and reeds, with pressed soil on top, in which they often placed shale or pebbles. Wood and reeds also built the roof, on which there was also pressed soil, acting as an insulator and ensuring coolness in summer and warm in winter.

The ground floor rooms were used as warehouses, workshops or mills, while the upper floors were the living quarters. In the richest houses, often the upper floor walls were decorated with murals. The streets were paved and the buildings' drainage was ensured through clay pipes lying in the walls and ending up in built sewers under the cobblestone streets.

The great number of murals found during the excavations is a valuable source of information on everyday life in Akrotiri, religion and the island's nature. They have been created basically with the technique of fresco, i.e. the work was executed on the still fresh plaster. This resulted in their colours remaining indelible. Often, however, the mortar dried out before the artist's work was completed, and he continued his work on a dry wall. At these points, the protection of the frescoes is done today by chemical means. Details were added later.

To the great surprise of scientists, the spectroscopic method revealed that the violet colour in details of the mural composition with the crocus collectors stems from the treatment of the sea snails that gave the Tyrian red. This proves that the level of the island's know-how and culture was particularly high. The themes of the wall paintings were particularly original. They were mostly inspired by the plant and animal world and there were also narrative scenes with people, mythological beings and deities. Among them were the so-called miniature frescoes, which were large-scale paintings (friezes) with small-sized figures placed high on the wall.

In almost all the excavated buildings, there were frescoes older than those that adorned their walls when the volcanic eruption took place. This shows that frescoes were an established way of decorating the interior, probably from the beginning of the 17th century BC.

The ash and pumice layer that covered the settlement after the eruption created the ideal environment of oxygen deficiency needed to preserve perishable materials. Thus, Akrotiri is one of the few places in Greece preserving testimonies about prehistoric arts such as furniture, wood carving, basketry and the construction of musical instruments, arts essentially unknown in modern research of the prehistoric Aegean or known only indirectly from depictions in art and references in Mycenaean records of Linear B writing.

The preservation of objects made of perishable materials in Akrotiri was in some cases facilitated by their partial charring. In cases where the materials were finally decomposed, cavities or prints of similar shape were often left in their place in the volcanic material. Filling such cavities with gypsum during the excavation recovers faithful casts of the decomposed objects.

The most important testimonies about the creation of perishable artifacts in Akrotiri are the bed casts, the cast of a table with sculpted legs, a pair of wooden percussion rattles with a relief of birds and crocuses and a large number of prints and charred pieces of knit baskets.

Due to the decomposition of organic materials, mainly of wood, used in the construction of buildings, the removal of volcanic deposits put the buildings at risk of collapse, so they had to be supported. During the excavations of Marinatos it was decided to inject reinforced concrete into the gaps created in the walls of the exposed buildings. In many cases of wooden door and window frames, the concrete was painted in brown, similar to wood, while knots were painted on it, so as to give the visitor an image as close as possible to that of the building before the eruption. In fewer cases, external support pilasters of reinforced concrete were constructed.

The findings of the excavations show that Akrotiri's society was not ruled by a monarch but by an elite operating in two main sectors, maritime trade and crafts, as agriculture in the surrounding area could not meet the needs of the large population. The ships of the frescoes seem capable of long journeys, while the port of Akrotiri had to be one of the most important of its time.

In fragments of inscriptions, extremely large quantities of fabrics are reported, which leads to the conclusion that the settlement was a place of gathering and processing of the wool produced by the neighbouring islands, probably Ios, Sikinos, Folegandros and Anafi. At the same time, wool fibers have been found in Akrotiri, which, according to laboratory analyses, are the oldest preserved proofs of the use of wool in the Mediterranean, except in the case of Egypt, where there are also similar findings.

The settlement's inhabitants had developed fire technology to a high degree and the use of fire is found in both houses and in economic and religious activities. Since the beginning of the third millennium BC, for example, the presence of permanent and portable cooking hobs and mobile or fixed ovens, ash and coal, trays, grills and sockets for skewers, braziers and flat plates for baking pies is detected. Findings also prove the cultivation of grapes and the production of wine.

The archaeological site is protected by a bioclimatic shelter of international fame, with excellent properties in controlling the area's climatic conditions, thanks to the volcanic ash that covers it. In summer, when the site receives the highest number of visitors and the ambient temperature is too high due to latitude and lack of vegetation, the shelter can lower the covered space's temperature by up to 8 degrees.

After the visit to Akrotiri, our journey to Santorini was completed and it was time to go home. We took the boat to Piraeus, convinced that even the most touristy place can become a revelation to the traveller who desires to go beyond the clichés and really explore it.

View of the archaeological site with its bioclimatic shelter

Above, the destroyed wooden frames of doors and windows had to be replaced by reinforced concrete, to preserve the buildings emerging through the excavation. Below, casts of beds

7 SERIFOS. A PARADISE OF AUTHENTICITY

A humble past and a more promising future

Few islands of the Cyclades have remained as authentic and as little spoiled by tourism as Serifos. This makes Serifos an ideal choice for those in search of a really calm and peaceful Cycladic island with traditional architecture and food and wonderful beaches, which are surprisingly numerous for the island's size.

In Greek mythology, Serifos is where Danaë and her infant son Perseus washed ashore. Her father Acrisius set them adrift at sea in a wooden chest in response to an oracle that his own grandson would kill him. When Perseus returned to Serifos with the head of the Gorgon Medusa, he turned Polydektes, the king of Serifos, and his retainers into stone as punishment for the king's attempt to marry his mother by force. Polydektes had sent Perseus in search of the head of Medusa, hoping that the hero would die in the expedition and thus Danaë would not have anyone to support her against the king's will.

The Cyclades occupied a prominent position in Prehistory, thanks to their central location in the Aegean Sea. The islands of the Aegean acted as a bridge uniting Europe to Asia and profited from the commercial activities between these lands, their ports receiving the ships which ensured that trade. The 3rd millennium BC, i.e. the Early Bronze Age, was the era of the so-called Cycladic civilization, which created the world-famous astonishing Cycladic figurines. These works of art in local white marble impress by their abstract forms, which inspired many modern artists. At that time the Cyclades had a dense population, installed in small settlements along the islands' coasts. However, Serifos doesn't seem to have experienced a particular prosperity, at least according to the archaeological findings to-date.

The settlements of the Cycladic civilization had a violent end, which resulted in the interruption of this artistic creation. Around 2000 BC, the Cyclades started being influenced by the Minoan civilization of Crete, the new emerging power in the Aegean Sea. That led to a new period of prosperity in the Cyclades, which ended with the decline of Crete around 1500 BC and the arrival of the Mycenaeans, who dominated the last phase of Bronze Age in Greece (Mycenaean period, 1600-1100 BC).

The Geometric period (900-700 BC) followed the two centuries of chaos engendered by the arrival of the Dorians in about 1100 BC and the subsequent fall of the Mycenaean civilization. Serifos is now mainly inhabited by Ionians who came from Attica.

In the Archaic period (7th – 6th century BC), which followed the

Geometric period, some islands experienced a new era of prosperity, but Serifos was a poor island. Serifos was one of the few islands which refused submission to Xerxes I, king of Persia. However, ancient writers almost always mention Serifos with contempt on account of its poverty and insignificance; and it was for this reason used by the Roman emperors as a place of exile. In antiquity, the island was proverbial for the alleged muteness of its frogs. In the Classical period all the Cyclades declined with the rise of Athens in the 5th century BC and their compulsory adhesion to the Athenian Alliance, which transformed them into Athens's satellites.

At the capital

The first contact of our hiking group with Serifos was at Livadi (Prairie), the port, and Chora, the island's capital overlooking it and connected with it via an easy trail, which, of course, we followed.

In 1207 Serifos became a minor dependency of the Venetian dukes of the Archipelago. The first of them, the Venetian nobleman Marco Sanudo, conquered most of the Cyclades after the fall of the Byzantine Empire to the crusaders of the 4th crusade and settled in Naxos. The Venetians re-used the ancient acropolis as a medieval castle. This crowns today's Chora, which, is, therefore, on the site of the ancient capital. However, few remains of it are visible today, among which worked blocks of island marble, and its main asset is the magnificent view it offers.

First images of Serifos. Chora, the capital above the port of Livadi

Chora of Serifos is a still well preserved fortified settlement of the Aegean. Here, more clearly than in other medieval settlements, you can distinguish the building system made for protection against pirate raids. The houses of the external ring are built attached to one another, without external openings at the time (that, of course, has changed), forming a protective wall

The port of Livadi, seen from Chora

Images from Chora at sunset

Like in all Cycladic settlements, also here whitewashed chapels are a characteristic feature of the built environment

The town hall of Serifos. A neoclassical 'dissonance' among the typical Cycladic traditional architecture. When Greece became an independent State in 1830, classicism was supposed to form the link with the ancient past. Therefore, public buildings were made according to this style and the upper classes adopted it with enthusiasm in their mansions. On the other hand, the rest of the population usually integrated some characteristic elements into the insisting traditional architecture, which was better adapted to the country's climate conditions and the owners' financial means. Since the Cyclades were islands of particularly restricted wealth, here neoclassical architecture was usually limited to public structures and very few houses of the most wealthy citizens. The exceptions were the islands of the ship-owners, Syros and Andros

At the monastery of the Archangels

After Chora, we visited the fortified monastery of the Taxiarches (the Archangels Michael and Gabriel). It was built in 1572 just outside the village of Galani. Like several other monasteries, it gives the exact image of a fortified medieval settlement, built for protection against pirates, more than today's villages. The latter have undergone the necessary changes for their adaptation to modern needs, such as the opening of larger windows and the creation of balconies on the walls of the outer ring, formerly blind or with extremely small windows. Moreover, other constructions have often been added beyond them. This often makes it difficult to distinguish the dense

198

initial medieval core. On the contrary, in this monastery you can easily imagine how these villages looked in the Middle Ages.

The monastery of the Taxiarches (Archangels), preserving the exact image of a medieval fortified settlement

Megalo Livadi. The industrial past at a fine beach

Our next stop was at Megalo Livadi (Great Prairie). In the late 19th century Serifos experienced a modest economic boom through the exploitation of the island's extensive iron ore deposits. The mines, situated in the area of Megalo Livadi, closed in the 1960s. It is curious that the ancient writers don't mention the iron and copper mines of Serifos. These were, however, exploited in antiquity, as existing traces demonstrate, and one might have supposed that they would have bestowed some prosperity upon the island. However, this didn't happen.

In the 20th century, the mines of Serifos were exploited by the mining company 'Société des mines de Seriphos-Spiliazeza', under the direction of German mineralogist Emile Grohmann. In the summer of 1916, in response to low pay, excessive working hours, poor safety conditions, and the company's refusal to rehire workers who had been drafted into the Greek army and recently demobilized, the 460 miners formed a union and organized a strike. Their leader was Konstantinos Speras, a Serifos native, who was an anarcho-syndicalist with long experience of labour struggles on the Greek mainland. Georg Grohmann, son of Emile who had died, asked for the help of Greek authorities, who sent 30 gendarmes from the nearby island of Kea. After detaining Speras and the strike committee, the gendarmerie lieutenant ordered his men to fire on the workers, who had gathered at the ore loading dock at Megalo Livadi and impended the loading of a cargo ship. Four workers were killed and a dozen wounded. The workers, aided by their wives, attacked the gendarmes with stones, killing three of them and routing the others. The freed leaders took control of island institutions and sent a message placing Serifos under protection of the French fleet at Milos. This effort at collective proletarian self-organization was cut short by the refusal of the French navy to intervene, and by the arrival of a Greek warship. Speras was arrested and charged with high treason, but released a few months later when the royalist government fell. Grohmann regained control of the mines, after granting improved working conditions and an 8-hour workday. This makes the miners' strike one of the major social events in 20th-century Greece.

Megalo Livadi

Remnants of the industrial past of Serifos in Megalo Livadi

Gyftika – Chora. A magnificent trail

This short trail offered us the most magnificent views of Chora. This book's cover photo and author photo are precisely from this trail.

Chora seen from the trail Gyftika - Chora

The ancient tower

The most impressive ancient monument in Serifos is the White Tower, a Hellenistic marble watchtower (dating from around 300 BC) with walls preserved to a height of 2 meters and an interior staircase. It stands on a hilltop just east of the road from Chora to Megalo Livadi. At least four other ancient towers have been located, including the megalithic Psaros Pyrgos or 'Couch of the Cyclops' in the island's southwest corner. The so-called 'Castle of the Old Woman' above Ganema and Koutalas preserves few remains of a collapsed dry-stone construction in a notch below the twin rocky summits.

The White Tower (around 300 BC)

Crossing the island. From Kentarchos to Chora

This trail, from the village of Kentarchos to Chora, crosses the eastern part of the island and offered us magnificent views to the sea, but also to the landscape of Serifos.

Above, the village of Kentarchos. Below, the port of Livadi

An astonishing work of art by nature on the trail from Kentarchos to Chora

One of the few dovecotes of Serifos, which came as a surprise, since they are not visible from the usual itineraries of visitors who don't hike. At my first visit to Serifos on my own, without the hiking group, I didn't even realise there were any dovecotes on the island

205

From Galani to Sykamia

The trail from the little village of Galani to the beach of Sykamia is another pleasant itinerary in Serifos, which offered us yet another opportunity to admire magnificent views. Thus our visit to this paradise of authenticity came to an end, with a strong desire to return.

Arriving at the beach of Sykamia from Galani. The island's green parts are almost exclusively such beds of streams forming little valleys and ending up at the coast

8 SIFNOS. PERFECT HARMONY OF NATURE AND ART

At the capital

You chose Sifnos for your summer holiday? You want to see it without suffering from the heat? A good proposal is to follow the trail from Artemonas to Kastro (Castle). It was Anna's idea and it proved to be a very good one. But first, let's see the island's heart, Chora.

Artemonas is part of the urban complex of Chora (the capital). Along with Apollonia, Ano Petali and Exambela. Each village has a different character and each one its own beauty. Artemonas is the most 'stately' settlement with neoclassical houses.

The others are more typical Cycladic villages, with irregular whitewashed houses. When Greece became an independent State in 1830, classicism was introduced by the Bavarian King Otto, a fervent admirer of ancient Greece. However, it was observed more faithfully by the upper class, who wanted to be 'modern' and 'European'. The people stayed attached to traditional architecture, which better served their everyday needs, occasionally adding neoclassical details in order not to stay excluded from the revival of ancient culture in its birthplace, as they saw classicism at the time.

What is a specific feature of Sifnos both in traditional and in neoclassical buildings is the addition of very sophisticated terracotta adornments, especially chimneys. Sifnos is the centre of development and diffusion of pottery in the Cyclades. The first samples of this art date from the Early Bronze Age (statuettes, decorative and handy articles). The abundance of raw materials in Sifnos (deposits of potter's clay) has helped in the development of this art.

At first, the potter's workshops were installed in the hinterland near Artemonas and Ano Petali, in order to be protected from pirates, who were dominating the Aegean. After the Greek independence and the elimination of piracy, they were transferred to the island's bays and especially to those protected from the strong north winds (meltem). Visitors can find traces of old potteries at villages by the seaside, such as Faros, Platys Gialos, Kamares and Vathy.

The artisans of Sifnos spread their art all over Greece, while many workshops were established by Sifnians or by others, who were their apprentices. Today, there are more than a dozen potter's workshops in Sifnos, contributing to the maintenance of the ancestral tradition.

Ano Petali, one of the villages composing Sifnos's capital (Chora)

Kato Petali, a bit further from the capital's complex

Artemonas, another one of the villages composing the island's capital. Sifnos has a long-standing pottery tradition. In the front left, one of the famous Sifnian chimneys, here with a decorative use

Artemonas. A triple church (Saint Constantine), common in the Cydades

Apollonia, the main village among the four composing the capital of Sifnos. A traditional laundry on the left

At the prehistoric acropolis of Aghios Andreas

Not far from Apollonia, you can visit the most important archaeological site in Sifnos: the Prehistoric acropolis (citadel) of Aghios Andreas (Saint Andrew).

The Cyclades occupied a prominent position in Prehistory, thanks to their central location in the Aegean Sea. The islands of the Aegean acted as a bridge uniting Europe to Asia and profited from the commercial activities between these lands, their ports receiving the ships which ensured that trade. The 3rd millennium BC, i.e. the Early Bronze Age, was the era of the so-called Cycladic civilization, which created the world-famous astonishing Cycladic figurines. These works of art in local white marble impress by their abstract forms, which inspired many modern artists. At that time the Cyclades had a dense population, installed in small settlements along the islands' coasts and Sifnos experienced a particular prosperity.

However, the settlements of the Cycladic civilization had a violent end, which resulted in the interruption of this artistic creation. Around 2000 BC, the Cyclades started being influenced by the Minoan civilization of Crete, the new emerging power in the Aegean Sea. That led to a new period of prosperity in the Cyclades, which ended with the decline of Crete around 1500 BC and the arrival of the Mycenaeans, who dominated the last phase of Bronze Age in Greece (Mycenaean period, 1600-1100 BC). The acropolis of Aghios Andreas was created at the end of that period, in the 13th century BC.

The Geometric period (900-700 BC) followed the two centuries of chaos engendered by the arrival of the Dorians in about 1100 BC and the subsequent fall of the Mycenaean civilization. Sifnos is now mainly inhabited by Ionians who came from Attica.

In the Archaic period (7th – 6th century BC), which followed the Geometric period, Sifnos acquired great wealth, thanks to its gold and silver mines, marble quarries and good quality terracotta vases. Moreover, with the use of a reamer, the Sifnians manufactured stone containers which, when filled with hot oil, obtained a dark colour and became very hard.

A testimony to the island's wealth is the treasury of the Sifnians, built in the sanctuary of Apollo in Delphi in about 525 BC. The treasuries were small buildings built in sanctuaries in the form of a temple where the Greek cities kept their offerings to the sanctuary's god. The treasury of the Sifnians was the most luxurious of all. It was made entirely of marble (partly from Sifnos) and adorned with a rich sculpted decoration (caryatid statues, pediment sculptures and a frieze) constituting a masterpiece of Archaic art.

Treasury of the Sifnians, around 525 BC, reconstitution by Theophil Hansen (1813-1891) (public domain work, {{PD-1923}})

However, this exceptional prosperity came to an abrupt end just after the construction of the treasury in Delphi, when Sifnos was invaded and destroyed by the island of Samos, one of the most powerful States in Archaic Greece. The Samians destroyed the island because the rich Sifnians refused to give them a loan of 10 talents. The Sifnians were obliged to pay the Samians 100 talents to make them leave Sifnos! Henceforth, Sifnos never recovered its former status and followed the fate of the rest of the Cyclades, which declined with the rise of Athens in the 5th century BC and their compulsory adhesion to the Athenian Alliance, which transformed them into Athens's satellites.

On the hill of Aghios Andreas, a strongly fortified citadel was established in the Mycenaean period. The double fortification wall was strengthened with eight rectangular towers that surrounded the acropolis. The town was also naturally fortified by the steep hill that also allowed for an excellent view in case enemies would come. The first excavation was conducted in 1898. Recent excavations have revealed most of the acropolis, as well as its complex defence system, which is unique in the Aegean.

It appears that there was human activity at the site also at the end of the Neolithic and in the Early Bronze Age (end of 4th millennium BC). The abandonment of the Mycenaean acropolis dates to the 11th century BC, at the time of the Dorian invasion.

The fortification wall was a very strong incentive for its re-occupation in historical times (second half of the 8th century BC). At that time, another wall and a large tower were added and two gateways were opened. Also from that time, the visitor can see the dense urban tissue and the system of evacuation of rain water. The settlement was eventually abandoned in the 4th century BC. Vessels and pottery from the different eras of habitation have also been unearthed. The site is one of the best examples of Mycenaean fortifications in the Cyclades and was one of the most important parts of the island's internal communication system with towers, some of which have been found.

The site was awarded in 2012 by the 'Europa Nostra' organization as a prototype of an excellent promotion of an ancient acropolis. But this location also offers a thrilling view of most of the island. The site is accessible on foot through a 45' climb of medium difficulty but is also easily accessible by car. The museum by the roadside offers very informative panels and valuable findings from antiquity to Byzantine times. The adjacent church of Aghios Andreas which gave the citadel its present name dates from the 17th century.

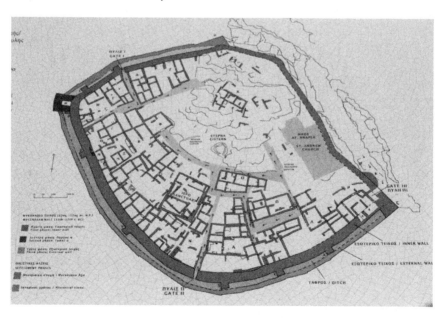

Map of the Prehistoric acropolis of Aghios Andreas, Zde / CC BY-SA (https://creativecommons.org/licenses/by-sa/4.0)

From Artemonas to Kastro

The trail from Artemonas leads to Kastro (castle), the medieval capital of Sifnos, built in the location of the ancient city. Its form dates mainly from the time of Venetian domination, a result of the 4th crusade. At the beginning of this period, Sifnos was part of the Duchy of the Archipelago, founded by the Venetian nobleman Marco Sanudo, with Naxos as its capital. Sanudo conquered most of the Cyclades in 1207 and incorporated them into his State. Sifnos was re-occupied by the Byzantine fleet for 38 years (1269-1307), and after a peace treaty with the Venetians the island was ceded to the Spaniard Giannoulis Dacoronia, a knight of Saint John, who proclaimed himself independent ruler of Sifnos and fortified the city.

The childless last descendant of the house of Dacoronia was succeeded by Nicholas Gozzadini, son of the ruler of Kythnos and Kea, Angelo Gozzadini. Sifnos was ceded in 1341 by the Duke of the Archipelago as fief to the noble Venetian Bertuccio Grimani, who never became the lord of the island. In 1537 Hayreddin Barbarossa, the admiral of the Ottoman fleet, conquered Sifnos which was reoccupied again in 1568, during the Turkish-Venetian war, by the Gozzadini who were made vassals to the Sublime Porte (the Sultan's court). In 1617 the rights of Angelo Gozzadini were revoked and the island was definitely annexed by the Ottoman Empire.

Since piracy was a great threat at the time, the inhabitants had gathered in the steepest part of the island. That was necessary to protect themselves from attacks. When the Greek State was created in 1830, piracy was eliminated. Then people started leaving the castle to live in less isolated locations.

The castle was built in the most inaccessible point. That's why its coast is very steep. So the trail runs alongside the cliffs. Thus, the water is very deep and its colour indescribable. And, as usual, at the most beautiful places, there is also a chapel. But in Sifnos chapels have an additional feature. The surrounding space, the precinct and the stairs leading there are all very elegantly arranged, more so than in other islands. We could say that here the coupling of nature and human intervention reaches an aesthetic summit.

You will have the opportunity to find out all this if you follow the trail from Artemonas to Kastro. First, you will encounter Panaghia Poulati (Virgin Mary of the birds). There you will be able to take the first dive.

In the course of your hike, you will see several places suitable for diving. We took advantage of all because it was very hot.

Our destination seen from the beginning of the trail

Panaghia Poulati

These walls are common in the Cyclades, where the scarce soil, vital to the inhabitants' survival, had to be retained by human intervention

At Kastro

Just before arriving at Kastro, you will see the cemetery and the beautiful churches of Saint John the Baptist and Saint Stephen. They are at the location of an important testimony to the more recent history of Sifnos. With the privileges granted by the Sultans Murad III (1580) and Ibrahim I (1646), Sifnos experienced a period of economic and social development. As in the rest of the Cyclades, the institution of self-government with the election of commissioners was developed.

An outcome of this situation was the foundation of the Common School in 1687 which operated in a dependency of the Holy Sepulchre of Jerusalem, located where the two churches stand today. The school was staffed by enlightened teachers and became known as the Koinon Paideuterion (Common Educational Institute) of the Archipelago, while it acquired a building complex for 300 students. Probably Josephus Moisiodakas, the great figure of the Greek Enlightenment, taught there. It functioned until 1833, when it was incorporated into the public educational system of the new Greek State as a Hellenic School.

Out of Kastro. Another sample of artistic sensitivity in the arrangement of the surrounding space. The cemetery with the churches of Saint John the Baptist and Saint Stephen, at the place where the Common Educational Institute of the Archipelago operated from 1687 to 1833

At the end of the trail, you will arrive at Kastro. Underneath you will see Eptamartyros, the church of the Seven Martyrs. You will visit it before or after Kastro. It will depend on how hot you feel. Here you will be able to take another dive.

Kastro is one of the best preserved fortified settlements of the Aegean. Here, more clearly than in other medieval settlements, you can distinguish the building system made for protection against pirate raids. The houses of the external ring are built attached to one another, without external openings at the time (that, of course, has changed), forming a protective wall. These were the narrow dwellings of the lower class. The members of the upper class built their much larger dwellings in the area created in the middle of the settlement, which was protected by the external walls of the smaller houses. Above the entrances of the upper class's dwellings we can still see the sculpted escutcheons of those families, mostly Venetian.

Eptamartyros. A perfect match of nature and human intervention

Traditional toilet in Kastro. All external wooden structures were added when the danger from pirates was over

A church of Kastro. A combination of whitewashed traditional architecture and
Venetian influences in the architectural details

In Cycladic architecture, buildings become sculptures in stone and lime

The castle is built in the place of the ancient city

A triple chapel

The re-use of ancient materials is common in settlements that are continuously inhabited

A 'window' from the introvert castle to the outer world

photo by Denis Roubien

Since the castle is built on the ancient city, antiquities can be found everywhere. If you wonder why they are not in a museum, in many cases it is preferred to let them in their original place, provided they cannot be taken

This is the Catholic church of Saint Anthony on the right, built by Giannoulis Dacoronia in the 14th century. That's why its Gothic elements are more evident. The presence of Catholic communities in many Cycladic islands is due to the long Venetian domination

And finally, there is Seralia, the 'port' of Kastro.

Seralia

To Chryssopighi

If this route seems too much for you, there is a lighter trail. From Faros to Chryssopighi. Here you will see the most famous church of Sifnos, with the island's biggest feast.

One thing is certain: whatever your choice, Sifnos offers great spots for diving. All with a natural and an artificial environment of incomparable beauty. As indeed is the whole island: of incomparable beauty.

9 SYROS. THE NOBLE HEART OF THE CYCLADES

A rare cultural jewel

On arrival at the harbour of Hermoupolis, the image seen by the visitor is the most typical of Syros: a large city that spreads wide and climbs on two hills. On the top of each hill a large church: the Resurrection on the right and Saint George on the left.

These two hills symbolise the special cultural identity of Syros: the Resurrection is Orthodox, Saint George is Catholic and they represent the two religious communities that inhabit the island.

On arrival at Syros by boat: on the left the hill of San Tzortzis with the church of Saint George, on the right the hill of Anastasia with the church of the Resurrection

At first sight, they look like two hills of about the same height, where Hermoupolis has climbed. In fact, however, the left hill is much taller. It's just more to the rear and its height is not visible. And it's not Hermoupolis going up on it. It's a medieval fortified town, seven centuries older than Hermoupolis. And completely, but completely different.

Hermoupolis is the largest neoclassical ensemble in Greece, founded only in 1822. It was once the largest city of the new Greek state, its largest port and its cultural capital. On the other hand, Ano Syros is one of the best preserved medieval fortified towns of the Aegean, founded in the 13th century. And moreover, it's one of the few that are still inhabited. This further increases its importance. Which, in any case, is particularly great because of its historical and architectural value.

Historical peculiarities

In 1207, three years after the crusaders of the Fourth Crusade occupied the Byzantine Empire, Marco Sanudo, a Venetian aristocrat, nephew of the doge Enrico Dandolo, occupied most of the Cycladic islands. He founded the Duchy of the Archipelago and settled in Naxos. This state included Syros. And then the cultural specificity of this island began being created...

When Greece was conquered by the crusaders, most of the inhabitants remained Orthodox. Catholicism was mostly represented by the feudal aristocracy of the conquerors. But Tinos and Syros are an exception to this rule. Here, the majority of the population embraced Catholicism. This was a long process that lasted throughout the Venetian domination and continued during the Ottoman domination after the conquest of the Cyclades by the Turks. This was practically done in 1537, with the attack of Hayreddin Barbarossa, the Ottoman Admiral-of-the-Fleet, and typically in 1566, when the last Duke of the Archipelago died. Then the islands officially joined the Ottoman Empire.

This historical development is reflected in the horizon of the fortified town through the monuments that stand out. Below the cathedral of Saint George, we see two historical monasteries: that of the Jesuits and that of the Capuchins. The dome of the former and the bell tower of the latter are typical landmarks in the outline of the hill of Ano Syros.

One would expect that these monasteries were founded during the Venetian domination. And yet not. They were founded during the Ottoman domination. The Venetians were always in great rivalry with the Pope and weren't favourable to the strengthening of the Catholic Church in their lands. Therefore, they didn't allow the establishment of Catholic monasteries. But when the Cyclades finally became Ottoman, in 1566, their Catholic populations were a good pretext for the French kings to intervene in the Ottoman Empire.

King Francis I had already signed a treaty in 1535 with Sultan Suleiman the Magnificent. According to it, all the Catholics of the empire would be under his protection. The French kings sent French monks and nuns who founded monasteries on many islands.

228

The hill of Ano Syros, crowned by the cathedral of Saint George. A little below and on the right is the dome of Our Lady of Mount Carmel of the Jesuit monastery, and farther down and on the right, the bell tower of Saint John of the Capuchin monastery

The Capuchins and Jesuits came to Syros in the 17th century. The Capuchins founded the monastery of Saint John in 1635, while the Jesuits settled permanently in Ano Syros and founded the monastery that includes the older church of Our Lady of Mount Carmel (1581) only in 1744. When France later changed its politics, the French were replaced by locals. They keep these institutions until today.

Some of them housed schools that later became so famous for offering good French education that they attracted students from as far as Madagascar, especially the Ursulines' schools in Naxos and Tinos. But originally they were the first schools in these islands since antiquity. Perhaps King Francis didn't have the most unselfish motives, but we must admit that he offered a great service to the Cyclades and beyond.

The initial schools no longer exist. However, the educational tradition continues by the Brothers of the Christian Schools (known as Frères), who keep their schools a little farther, at the border with Hermoupolis.

Ano Syros and Hermoupolis

This French protection had a consequence of great historical significance for modern Greece: it became the cause of the creation of Hermoupolis, the urban, economic, industrial and cultural centre of 19th-century Greece.

With the destruction of Chios by the Turks in 1822, during the Greek Revolution, many refugees came to Syros because, due to the old treaty that protected the areas with Catholic populations, the Turks could not harm them here.

They were followed by the inhabitants of the destroyed islands of Psara and Kasos in 1824 and many others from different regions of Greece and Asia Minor. All of them settled in the previously uninhabited port of Syros, under the medieval settlement, which until then was simply called Chora or Apano (upper) Chora.

So, until 1822, Ano Syros was the island's only settlement. Piracy that plagued the Aegean made the inhabitants gather at the top of the steep rock so that all together they would be able to cope better with them. The limited space resulting from this concentration forced the inhabitants to find solutions to create room for everyone. Thus, the houses were extended over the street and created the 'stegadia' or 'steadia', namely, the covered passageways, over which there are rooms of neighbouring houses.

Entering Ano Syros

Although it's impossible to get to Ano Syros without going through Hermoupolis, we will start from the former. Thus, you will visit the sights chronologically and understand them better.

After entering Ano Syros, you will soon be on the main street, Piazza. Here are all the stores.

The church of Saint Sebastian. The only parish church of this saint in Greece

Entering Ano Syros. One of the many 'stegadia', providing extra space from above. This was necessary in the confined space of a medieval settlement, where the houses were attached to one another in order to create a wall for protection against pirates

At the house of Markos Vamvakaris

And a surprise for many: walking in Ano Syros you will definitely stumble upon the house where its most famous child was born: the rebetiko's leading composer, Markos Vamvakaris. Today his home is a museum and you can visit it.

The house - museum of Markos Vamvakaris. The great composer of rebetiko was born here

Another one of the many 'stegadia', at the Capuchin monastery

The first historical monument: the Capuchin monastery

The church of Saint John, of the Capuchin monastery. In its yard, the elders met during the Ottoman domination. The underground crypts of the church provided shelter during pirate raids

One of the rare cases where we see a sahnisin (wooden closed balcony) in a place where wood is scarce

photo by Denis Roubien

A typical particularly narrow 'stegadi'. The bell tower of the Capuchin monastery is visible behind it

A very rare case of a wooden and even elaborate shelter. Obviously a neoclassical addition after Independence

A particularly impressive 'stegadi'

Traditional ceilings are covered with 'fides' (snakes), a local kind of cedar

The cathedral of Saint George

Ano Syros on the left and Hermoupolis on the right. View from the chapel of Kioura of Plaka

Kioura (Lady) of Plaka (1686). From here you will see the view to the rock of Ano Syros and Hermoupolis

Climbing to Saint George from the back of the settlement. On the right, Saint Michael Taxiarchis

Saint George as seen looking from below

The next historical monument: the Jesuit monastery

The church of Our Lady of Mount Carmel of the Jesuit monastery. It was built in 1581. The marble façade dates from 1824, which makes it one of the oldest marble constructions of such scale in modern Greece

The last and most impressive historical monument: the cathedral of Saint George

Cathedral of Saint George. It was rebuilt after many disasters in 1652. Its current form arose from the renovation of 1832-1834

At the top of the hill of San Tzortzis, you will see the trademark of the fortified town and emblematic image of the island for centuries, when there was only Ano Syros. It's of great historical importance since it's the seat of the Catholic bishop, next to the building of the Catholic Diocese of Syros, where the island's oldest archives are preserved for centuries. But it was also the last stronghold against pirate raids since it's also the settlement's highest point.

The church of the Holy Trinity (1604)

photo by Denis Roubien

252

Ano Syros today

Unfortunately, the change in the way of life has made the narrow streets of Ano Syros and its small houses unfit to the increased demands of today's humans. Result: from 6,000, which was the population of Ano Syros for centuries, now there are only a few hundred inhabitants. Most of them left for Athens or went down to Hermoupolis. However, the efforts to get Hermoupolis and Ano Syros to join UNESCO's World Heritage List are optimistic messages for the future.

For the moment, you make the effort to go up there, walk through its streets, visit its monuments and enjoy the view from the balconies of the restaurants and cafés. Looking at the sea, which no longer brings pirates, but visitors who are flocking more and more to this island of enormous cultural density.

A concentrated Greece

In the background, Ano Syros, crowned with the Catholic cathedral of Saint George, was the only settlement on the island until 1822. Hermoupolis was then created at its foot

The title of this chapter may seem exaggerated to you. However, you will change your mind if you learn the history of Hermoupolis. As we said,

253

for centuries, Syros had only the medieval settlement of Ano Syros. The area underneath was empty, a wasteland, like the whole island.

Until 1822, when refugees fleeing the Turks who were destroying resurrected areas benefited from the island being protected by the kings of France and started settling in the wasteland.

The hill of Anastasia, with the Orthodox church of the Resurrection (Anastasis) as a 'counterweight' to the Catholic Saint George of Ano Syros

All these brought the knowledge and specialities for which their regions were distinguished. Thus, Hermoupolis became a kaleidoscope and a miniature of all Hellenism: a concentrated Greece, which gathered in a small space all the characteristics of the most distinguished Greeks, since the most creative and those who fought the most for their survival arrived here.

That's why Hermoupolis embodies the modern Greek miracle of survival and creativity. Within a few years, and for many decades afterwards, Hermoupolis became the largest city of the Greek state, which was created in the meantime. Moreover, it was a candidate for capital, and the main reason for its rejection was the absence of a hinterland on such a small island. But it was not just the largest city. Due to the special features of its settlers, it immediately became the largest commercial and cultural centre of Greece.

Miaouli Square. The former heart of Greece

Perhaps the most eloquent testimony of the greatness that Hermoupolis has known is its central square, former Otto Square and today Miaouli Square. The buildings that surround it constitute one of Greece's most magnificent architectural ensembles. Suffice it to compare the Town Hall, the work of the German architect Ernst Ziller, with the Athens Town Hall, built at the same time, to understand the position of Hermoupolis in 19th-century Greece. It's the grandest town hall in the whole country (with its current limits) and one of its most impressive public buildings. And of course, like most of Hermoupolis, it's neoclassical.

When Greece became an independent State in 1830, classicism was introduced by the Bavarian King Otto, a fervent admirer of ancient Greece. However, it was observed more faithfully by the upper class, who wanted to be 'modern' and 'European'. The people stayed attached to traditional architecture, which better served their everyday needs, occasionally adding neoclassical details in order not to stay excluded from the revival of ancient culture in its birthplace, as they saw classicism at the time. Hermoupolis having been once the most important city in Greece, the 'official' classicism is more frequent here than in most other Greek cities, making Hermoupolis second only to Athens in that respect.

The town hall houses also the Archaeological Museum with very important findings, especially from Prehistory. The Cyclades occupied a prominent position in Prehistory, thanks to their central location in the Aegean Sea. The islands of the Aegean acted as a bridge uniting Europe to Asia and profited from the commercial activities between these lands, their ports receiving the ships which ensured that trade. The 3rd millennium BC, i.e. the Early Bronze Age, was the era of the so-called Cycladic civilization, which created the world-famous astonishing Cycladic figurines. These works of art in local white marble impress by their abstract forms, which inspired many modern artists. At that time the Cyclades had a dense population, installed in small settlements along the islands' coasts and Syros experienced a particular prosperity.

However, the settlements of the Cycladic civilization had a violent end, which resulted in the interruption of this artistic creation. Around 2000 BC, the Cyclades started being influenced by the Minoan civilization of Crete, the new emerging power in the Aegean Sea. That led to a new period of prosperity in the Cyclades, which ended with the decline of Crete around 1500 BC and the arrival of the Mycenaeans, who dominated the last phase of Bronze Age in Greece (Mycenaean period, 1600-1100 BC).

The two most important sites which gave most of the prehistoric findings are Kastri and Chalandriani, in the northern, almost uninhabited part of the island. Kastri is a settlement dating from 2800-2300 BC. It was possibly here that Syros was inhabited for the first time. South of Kastri is the small settlement of Chalandriani, where a prehistoric acropolis (fortress) has been excavated, as well as a large cemetery, from where most of the findings come.

The Geometric period (900-700 BC) followed the two centuries of chaos engendered by the arrival of the Dorians in about 1100 BC and the subsequent fall of the Mycenaean civilization. Syros is now mainly inhabited by Ionians who came from Attica.

In the Archaic period (7th – 6th century BC), which followed the Geometric period, some islands experienced a new era of prosperity, but Syros was a relatively poor island. In the Classical period all the Cyclades declined with the rise of Athens in the 5th century BC and their compulsory adhesion to the Athenian Alliance, which transformed them into Athens's satellites.

Miaouli Square. The Town Hall (1875-1891)

To the left of the Town Hall. The Ladopoulos building (1870), housing the Historical Archives of Hermoupolis

To the right of the Town Hall. The 'Hellas' club, today the Cultural Centre of the municipality. It was designed by the Italian architect Pietro Sampo and built in 1862-1863

The music platform (another testimony of the high cultural level of Hermoupolis) in Miaouli Square and the statue of the homonymous admiral from Hydra

'Apollo' theatre. Testimony of a high culture

The other testimony of the greatness of Hermoupolis and its high cultural level is the 'Apollo' Theatre. It was designed by Pietro Sampo (like the 'Hellas' club) and built in 1862-1864. It was modelled on the famous Italian opera theatres, as opera was then at its zenith in Europe. Great names of the international artistic firmament appeared here.

Great personalities of art are depicted on the roof of the 'Apollo' Theatre

The environment of the 'Apollo' Theatre is worthy of it

Vaporia. The grandeur of the Greek navy

Moving beyond Miaouli Square, to the north, we reach Vaporia (ships). The name of this neighbourhood testifies to the occupation of its inhabitants: ship owners, who, of course, constituted an important component of that time's society, since the first settlers came from naval islands.

The church that dominates Vaporia is Saint Nicholas the Rich. It's called so as to stand out from Saint Nicholas the Poor of Ano Syros. The church of the ship owners' quarter could not, of course, have been devoted to another saint.

The dome of Saint Nicholas the Rich

The façade of Saint Nicholas the Rich

The mansions of Vaporia forming the sea front

A sample of Palladian style (from the great Renaissance architect Andrea Palladio, who became a pan-European model), perhaps unique in Greece

All Hermoupolis a unique neoclassical ensemble

But what is characteristic of Hermoupolis is that the sights are not limited to a small number of buildings. Here you will see the largest neoclassical ensemble in the world, a unique spectacle.

Tsiropina Square, where we can find the Prefecture of the Cydades

264

265

The Virgin Mary of Psara. The boat church

If you leave the centre of Hermoupolis, to the south, in the opposite direction in relation to Vaporia, you will reach Psariana, the district of the refugees from Psara who arrived here in 1824. A monument you should not miss here is the church of the Assumption of the Virgin, known as the Virgin Mary of Psara (Panaghia Psarianon), built by the refugees in 1828-1829. It's a church probably unique in Greece.

You may have heard that this church houses an icon, work of El Greco. This image is particularly valuable because it's one of his few surviving works dating before leaving Greece, when he still painted according to the Byzantine tradition of the Cretan School. A very different style from the one he is world-famous for. But, apart from this treasure, this church also hides others, unique in Greece.

The last time I found myself at Syros was during a conference. At the intervals, I engaged myself in systematically taking photos of the neoclassical houses, something I hadn't been able to do before. For five days I was taking photos for hours, covering the entire complex of Hermoupolis and Ano Syros. During my wanderings, I found the Virgin Mary of Psara. Knowing that there, is the icon of El Greco, I went in to see it.

The icon is in the narthex, so after having seen it, I proceeded to the nave. Then I went out without observing anything special because I didn't look above the door. Also, I did not meet anyone. That was important.

Shortly before the ship's departure, one last walk and one last look at El Greco's icon. If you consider how scarce his works are in Greece (less than ten), you will understand why I went back there (it's not close, it's on the other side of the city centre). This time, however, the church was not empty.

There was Father Konstantinos, the vicar, who excitedly related the accidental discovery of the icon in 1983, under layers of varnish that made it seem an ordinary icon with no particular value. The discovery was due to the observation of an archaeologist, who suspected what was hidden beneath the varnish. Father Konstantinos, already then the church's vicar, was present at the event and even after all these years he will narrate to you the discovery with great emotion. But there's also something else he will tell you and show you with enthusiasm.

As Father Konstantinos will explain to you, since the inhabitants of Psara were famous sailors, their technical knowledge was much better in the construction of ships rather than buildings. The buildings of Psara were simple and humble. Their ships, however, were proportional to the island's great naval power.

The Dormition of the Virgin, by El Greco. Church of the Virgin Mary of Psara (public domain work, {{PD-1923}})

So, Father Konstantinos will reveal to your stunned eyes a church that was built as a boat. First, he will show you the gallery. Instead of the familiar balcony with bars, you will see the stern of a ship, only instead of a mermaid, it has God the Father painted in its centre! That's what I hadn't noticed coming out of the church last time.

The pulpit is of a similar construction, although less apparent. But you will not find the boat only at the gallery and the pulpit. If you are not afraid of heights and precarious creaking wooden ladders, the agile Father Konstantinos will run up the scary rickety staircase to the interior of the roof, prompting you to follow him. Although he's over sixty, prepare for a run to catch up with him. When at last you will manage to reach the top of the ladder and look through, over the roof of the interior of the church, you will not believe your eyes.

The gallery, in the form of the stem of a ship

The ceiling in form of an overturned hull of a boat

You will see a whole hull of a boat, overturned. This was the most robust wooden structure the people from Psara knew how to make and that's what they did. Don't forget that we are talking about a time when it was difficult to build a large church with a wooden roof and no dome.

In Greece, such roofs were unknown. In Hermoupolis, you will see the only example I know (and even that I didn't know) so far. Who could believe that Syros, overloaded with treasures, has still more treasures to reveal? After five days of wandering, just one last walk before boarding revealed new treasures. So, wander as much as you can, look around and talk with those who are willing to talk to you. You may run into wonderful people who will reveal wonderful things to you.

photo by George Roubia

The pulpit

Remnants of the industrial past

Going farther south, after Psariana, you will meet an impressive array of industrial buildings of a spectacular scale in relation to the island's size. Undeniable witnesses to the great industrial development that Syros has known, they are now dilapidated, testifying to the decline that followed when Piraeus became the main port of Greece. Some have found a new use, such as the Industrial Museum. Others patiently wait to be given a new destination, which will save them from abandonment and decay.

photo by Denis Roubien

The resting place. Even here Hermoupolis stands out

On the same side of the city, another witness to the wealth that Hermoupolis experienced in the 19th century is also the resting place of its inhabitants. There are two cemeteries, the Orthodox and the Catholic one. Since the Orthodox population included all ship owners and rich merchants, the Orthodox cemetery is the one that contains the most impressive burial monuments. Here, the sculptors of Tinos, the centre of marble craftsmanship of modern Greece, had the opportunity of creating many of the works that make them worthy heirs of Phidias.

To understand what cultural wealth we are talking about, think that the photos you see are a small selection. Only an on-site visit will give you the full picture of this modern Greek miracle called Hermoupolis.

10 TINOS. THE LAST JEWEL IN THE CROWN OF VENICE

Tinos. For how many days?

'You are staying five days in Tinos?!' Said the middle-aged lady in the hotel restaurant to Fani, a member of our hiking group. 'What are you going to do here five entire days? You will visit the Virgin Mary, you will eat a galaktoboureko at Pyrgos, and then what?'

She couldn't imagine that, for us, five days would not be enough to discover the most misunderstood island of the Cyclades. And yet, it's the most visited one. It has more visitors annually than Mykonos and Santorini, its world-famous neighbours. It seems incredible, but it has a simple explanation.

Almost all visitors who flock to Tinos do as our astonished hotel acquaintance: they go for a pilgrimage to the most celebrated religious destination of Greece: Megalochari, the Virgin Mary of the Great Grace. They usually descend from the ship and go immediately to the church. After the necessary time in it, a short stop at one of the main avenue's shops to buy a souvenir, usually the icon of their favourite saint. And then back to the boat and to Piraeus, after a 5-hour trip. Often without spending the night on the island, in order to minimise the cost.

Megalochari, the Virgin Mary of the Great Grace, on its celebration day, 25th of March. The greatest pilgrimage in Greece

276

A little beyond Megalochari

The most adventurous ones go as far as making the classic short tourist trip. First, a visit to the convent of Kechrovouni, to pay homage to the nun-saint Pelaghia.

The best preserved medieval settlement, with no subsequent additions. In fact, it's the convent of Kechrovouni

In 1823, during the Greek Revolution, Pelaghia said she had a vision. The Virgin Mary revealed to her that an icon of hers was on a hill next to the port. Sure enough, the icon was found there and a sumptuous shrine emerged at the same place immediately afterwards. The Greeks considered this to be a favourable omen for the outcome of the Revolution. Thus, the icon became the most venerated religious object in Greece.

After the convent, perhaps a visit to Pyrgos, the only village known to more than a few people. Apart from its beauty, it owes its fame to its great marble sculptors. They have created some of the best works of art of modern Greece. There, in the little village square, under the shade of trees, they will taste the famous galaktoboureko mentioned by our acquaintance, a sweet filled with cream.

But even those who venture to Pyrgos, at the other end of the island, soon return to their boat. To go back home and be able thereafter to say that they, too, have visited the sacred island.

Kostas, the chief of our group, smiled indulgently when he heard the comment that could have been said by almost anyone of the island's visitors. "Tinos has about forty old villages, but we will traverse 'only' 24 of them. All of them are beautiful, but, unfortunately, they are not all suitable for hiking", he said. Since he has been hiking in Greece for decades, always adding new destinations to the souvenir album of his adepts, we had to take his word for it.

That's another surprise. Forty old villages? If you open any book on the Aegean islands and especially the Cyclades, you will always read the same thing: that, for centuries, the few inhabitants that survived the continuous pirate attacks had to nestle on the most inaccessible rock, to save their lives. In most islands, they were no more than a few hundred, so they had to stick together in one village. In the largest islands, they afforded to build a little more than one. But forty? That sounds incredible.

Historical explanations

You already suspect something is different on this island. If you want to understand it, Father Markos is your best option. Whether you prefer to read his books before coming, in order to surprise your unsuspecting travel mates, or you prefer a personal contact.

I preferred the latter and learned a lot of interesting things. He is probably the island's most prolific historian and responsible for the archives of the Catholic Archdiocese of Naxos and Tinos. Yes, that's right. A Catholic Archdiocese in the island housing the greatest Greek Orthodox pilgrimage, in a country of an overwhelming Orthodox majority. Again, there is a perfectly good explanation.

In 1207, three years after the crusaders of the fourth crusade conquered the Byzantine Empire, Marco Sanudo, a Venetian nobleman, nephew of the doge Enrico Dandolo, seized most of the Cyclades. He created the Duchy of the Archipelago and settled in Naxos.

Tinos and Mykonos, though, were not part of this state. That same year they came under the two Venetian brothers Andrea and Geremia Ghisi and their heirs. That lasted until 1390 when Venice undertook their direct administration. The rest of the Cyclades were conquered by the Ottomans in 1537 and officially annexed by the Ottoman Empire in 1566, with the death of the last Duke of the Archipelago. But Venice managed to keep Tinos until as late as 1715. That was partly thanks to Xobourgo, the highest fortress of the Aegean, 641 metres high.

Needless to say, from up there we had a magnificent view. Not only the whole island could be seen, but also many others around it. Thanks to Xobourgo, Tinos became Venice's last possession in the Aegean. And, by extension, the last bastion of the Western world in the Eastern Mediterranean.

Above, the highest fortress of the Aegean. Thanks to it, Venice kept Tinos for more than five centuries. Xobourgo with the village of Tripotamos at its feet. Below, looking down from Xobourgo. Xinara

Looking down from Xobourgo. Koumaros and, in the background, Volax

Looking far away from Xobourgo. Ktikados. Since Ktikados is a mixed village, two churches dominate its horizon: on the left the Orthodox one of Panaghia Megalomata and on the right the Catholic one of the Holy Cross

An island of a special cultural identity

When Greece was conquered by the crusaders, most of the inhabitants remained Orthodox. Catholicism was mostly represented by the feudal aristocracy of the conquerors. But Tinos and Syros were an exception to that rule. Here, the majority of the population followed the conquerors' religion. And although this is well known for Syros, very fewer people know the case of Tinos.

That's because the bulk of Syros's mixed population lives in its port. And since this is also the capital of the Cyclades, it makes the particularity of Syros too obvious to be missed. On the contrary, this part of Tinos's identity is to be found in a constellation of villages, well hidden from the uninitiated eye in the island's interior. The second reason is that the pilgrimage to Megalochari almost eclipsed anything else.

Since my aim is to present less known aspects of known destinations, we will first focus on the Inner Parts of Tinos (Mesa Meri). That's the island's central and eastern portion, containing most of the medieval villages. Their name is in opposition to the island's farthest side, the Outer Parts (Exo Meri). The Inner Parts are additionally divided into the Upper and the Lower Parts (Pano Meri and Kato Meri).

'How many of you live here?' One of our group asked the old man who came out of his house to greet us at the little village of Loutra (Baths). 'Ten at this moment. Many more will come from Easter onward'.

It's late March and we suspect that what we see is the ordinary image of this village most of the year. We got similar answers in every other village, apart from some large ones, like Komi, Triantaros or Falatados. Most of the island's inhabitants have moved mainly to Athens. They come here only in summer if they still work, or from Easter to early fall if they have retired.

And yet, Tinos had once as many as 28,000 inhabitants, when Naxos, the archipelago's largest island, had no more than 6,000, according to old times' travellers. Who could imagine that Loutra, this village of ten permanent inhabitants had once a world-famous girls' school of as many as 300 pupils?

A school of international range

The explanation of these overwhelming numbers is again to be found in the island's history. After the Cyclades became Ottoman, at last, their Catholic population was a good pretext for King Francis I of France to interfere in the Ottoman Empire. He had already signed a treaty with Sultan Suleiman the Magnificent. According to it, all the Catholics of the Empire would be under his protection. That partly explains why Tinos acquired such a population. Because it became a shelter for the persecuted from all over Greece.

The French kings sent French monks and nuns, who founded monasteries and convents in many islands. When France later changed its politics, the French were replaced by locals. They keep these institutions until today. Some of them housed schools. These became later so famous for offering good French education, that they attracted pupils from as far as Madagascar. But at their beginning, they were the first schools in these islands since ancient times. Perhaps King Francis didn't have the most selfless motives. But we have to admit that he offered a great service to the Cyclades and not only them.

In Tinos, that school was precisely at Loutra and administered by the Ursulines. The convent exists still, but the school fell, alas, victim to the massive move of the inhabitants to Athens after World War II. The nuns continue their educational tradition in the new schools they founded in the capital and the school at Loutra became a museum. There, guided by a local girl, we discovered the incredibly high level of education it once offered to its pupils.

Loutra. The convent of the Ursulines, with its world-famous girls' school

But the small village of Loutra has yet more to offer. It wasn't only the Ursulines who observed its beauty, but also the Jesuits. Their large monastery of Saint Joseph has a museum of folk art. In it, we discovered an astonishing collection of tools, agricultural equipment and much more. Among its exhibits, no one overlooked the 'machine' of making 'petroto', the island's exquisite cheese. During the production procedure, it is pressed with a heavy stone (petra in Greek), which explains its name.

Above, Loutra. Convent of the Ursulines. The painting classroom. Below, a monumental urban ensemble amid the fields. Jesuit monastery of Saint Joseph at Loutra. In the background, Krokos

Perfectly preserved medieval settlements

Apart from their religious buildings, the medieval villages of Tinos are typical Cycladic settlements. But usually of the most beautiful kind.

In the village of Dyo Choria (which actually means Two Villages) I remembered what I had read in a history book. An eighteenth-century British traveller had reported that when he arrived here, he had to have his mule unloaded. Otherwise, it could not pass through the village's main street. He asked the locals what was the fastest way for him to traverse the village. And they advised him to go from one roof to the other. And in fact, that's where most of them were at the moment, participating in a celebration since the village had literally no open space.

For protection against pirates, the locals built their houses attached to one another. Thus, they formed a continuous outer front, with no openings, like a fortification. The lack of space was such, that they even built parts of their houses above the streets.

The ideal place to see how the Cycladic settlements were at the time of piracy, when they were not whitewashed, so that they couldn't be seen, is Monastiria, because it's an abandoned village. The only 'dissonance' is the church of Saint Joseph

Monastiria

Monastiria

An elegant solution to the scarcity of space in medieval villages. Loutra

Another elegant solution to the scarcity of space in medieval villages. Xinara

Above, a kapasos (chimney made of an upside down pot) in Komi. Below, one of the countless auxiliary buildings decorating the countryside of Tinos. Near Perastra, at the trail Loutra - Perastra - Komi

The huge slabs of Tinos allow even the construction of ceilings. Tarabados

Kampos, as seen from the trail from Tarabados. One of the settlements that preserved their compact character

Discovering the hospitality of Tinos

All the island's medieval villages are still like this, but they are usually surrounded by more recent and more aerated parts. That gives a false impression that what the British traveller describes no longer exists. That was our first impression when we arrived at the main square of Dyo Choria, immediately out of the dense medieval core.

It was then that a hospitable lady materialised from nowhere, bringing a jug of home-made lemonade along with cups, enough for the whole group, about fifteen people. She was the only living soul we saw in this large village, but appearances were deceptive. Wherever we went, there were always people coming out of their houses to greet us. They all seemed very happily surprised to see visitors when they least expected them. Some of them offered us treats, like dates at Tripotamos and chocolates at Kardiani.

The most beautiful houses for... non-humans

Beautiful houses are not to be found only in villages, but also out of them. Out of the village of Tarabados, we came across perhaps the most enviable ensemble of massive housing for... non-humans.

I am of course talking of the famous dovecotes of Tinos, which are said to be more than one thousand. They are to be found all over the Inner Parts, but Tarabados offers the greatest concentration of them. Moreover, there is a long trail going along them. Following that trail, we exclaimed more than once how lucky these pigeons are, to live in such houses. Until they are eaten, of course, we thought afterwards. Anyway, when I showed photos of them to foreign colleagues of mine, they couldn't believe these constructions are made for pigeons. They told me they seemed to them too luxurious even for humans.

The most enviable ensemble of massive housing for... non-humans. At the trail of the dovecotes at Tarabados

Tarabados again

Humans and pigeons lodging together. Berdemiaros

Mountados. At the trail Mountados - Sbirados - Tripotamos

Maybe Tarabados offers the most spectacular ensemble of dovecotes. However, the prize for the most beautifully situated must go to an isolated one, midway at the trail to Agapi (the Greek word for 'love'). The small waterfall at its feet makes it really unique. Yes, a waterfall. The arid Cyclades, when visited in winter or spring, after a period of rain, can have even waterfalls.

A waterfall in the Cyclades. Near Agapi, **at the trail Volax - Agapi**

Modernism in the Middle Ages

Afterwards, the trail led us to a valley of many more dovecotes and the village of Agapi at its end. And behind our backs, dominating the valley, we saw the most modernist medieval church you can imagine.

It's the chapel of Saint Sophia, supposed to date from the 10th century. Apart from its very interesting interior mural paintings, the exterior looks as if it were the very inspiration of Le Corbusier, the famous modernist Swiss architect.

In his writings, he claims that the whitewashed chapels he saw in the Cyclades inspired him greatly in his work, especially the chapel of Notre Dame du Haut in Ronchamp, France. However, I very much doubt he ever saw this particular chapel. Hiking in hidden valleys of Tinos was very unlikely to come to his mind as a means of discovering the island.

Agapi, the valley with the dovecotes, as we arrive from Volax

Saint Sophia at Agapi, at the trail from Volax. Le Corbusier would have loved this 10th-century modernist church

More the pity, since he would no doubt have been thrilled by the harmonic asymmetry of its façade. In my opinion, this is a masterpiece of abstract art and, I have to admit, my favourite church in Tinos. Maybe this doesn't do justice to the monumental Baroque churches of the Inner Parts or to the marble masterpieces of the Outer Parts that you can see even in the smallest village, but there it is.

The magnificence of the Italian Baroque in little Tinos

And that's another curious thing. Among the island's thousand churches (as many as the dovecotes), most rural chapels are the well-known whitewashed cubes so enthusiastically described by Le Corbusier.

But the large parish churches in the villages seem to come from another part of the planet. To be exact, they come from Italy. Italy gave the religious architectural models not only to the Catholics of Tinos but often also to their Orthodox neighbours, especially in mixed villages.

At first sight, the most impressive example is the cathedral of the Virgin Mary of the Rosary. This is in the particularly beautiful village of Xinara (which means big fountain in the local vocabulary).

A small village with an unexpectedly majestic church. Saint John in Skalados. Probably the oldest tall bell tower of Tinos (1792). Opposite, the village of Smardakito

A large Baroque cathedral amid the fields. The Virgin Mary of the Rosary at Xinara

The façade of the cathedral of the Virgin Mary of the Rosary at Xinara

Saint Zachary in Kalloni. Many say it's the largest church in Tinos (photo by Markisia Armaou)

A bit of Baroque Rome in the heart of the Cydades. Saint Anne at Perastra. At the trail Loutra - Perastra - Komi. Below, a house in Komi. A very rare appearance of Baroque in secular architecture

Not only Baroque but also leaning. Karkados, Transfiguration. Also known as little Pisa

A rare and very interesting coupling of 'formal' and traditional architecture.
Pilgrimage of the Sacred Heart in Xobourgo (initially monastery of the Jesuits until
their installation in Loutra). The elegant traditional little dome at the side aisle
constitutes a 'melodic dissonance' in the strict formal architecture of the whole

The Presentation of the Virgin Mary in Tripotamos. In Tinos, even Orthodox churches are often Baroque

Panaghia Megalomata (large-eyed-Virgin-Mary) in Ktikados. Another Orthodox church with Baroque influences

But I think that the most important example of this influence is not that obvious.

An unknown masterpiece

Franciscan monastery of Saint Anthony of Padua. The usual for Tinos Baroque façade hides a surprise

If you are really intrigued, don't lose the opportunity to visit the Franciscan church of Saint Anthony of Padua at Chora, the port. Don't stop at its façade and say 'Oh my God, I can't take any more Baroque! I came here to see a simple Cycladic island with just a whitewashed village and beaches and I keep seeing monuments everywhere!'

Instead, go inside and turn to the left. There, you will see a miniature of Michelangelo's Laurentian Library in Florence. Observe the quality of the work and think of the date of its completion: 1747, when most of Greece was occupied by the Ottomans and almost completely cut-out from the rest of Europe. That will persuade you that this island must have been a cultural hub.

And if the church is closed, don't hesitate to ask from the Catholic Archdiocese, next to it, to send someone to open it for you. That's what we did and a very kind lady from Kalloni opened the church for us. Don't forget, the hospitality of this island's inhabitants is beyond description.

The little sister of Michelangelo's Laurentian Library. Saint Anthony of Padua at Chora

The hidden beauty of Chora

To reward you for the trouble you took to discover this place, one of my personal favourites, I will give you a tip. Behind this Franciscan monastery extends Pallada, Chora's most beautiful quarter. I assure you it will change your mind if you thought this insular capital city is less attractive than others. There, among some very beautiful neoclassical houses, you will find some very good restaurants offering the island's delicious local food. Don't miss the famous artichokes and louza, the local salted pork. The local cheese goes without saying.

Who said the capital city of Tinos is not that attractive? Wrong!

Chora, Saint Nicholas

From Mexico to Tinos

Back to the island's interior, I advise you to let your steps lead you to Pentostrato, next to the villages of Mesi and Steni. There, you will find another unique church. I know you can't take more Baroque than a normal human being in such a short time. But this one is different. I will hint that it's a kind of church unique not only in Greece but perhaps in the whole of Europe.

A Mexican church lost in the Cyclades. Saint Francis at Pentostrato

Does it intrigue you to see a Mexican church in the middle of a Cycladic island? Then don't miss the 18th-century Franciscan monastery of Saint Francis. It looks nothing like anything else around it. For mysterious reasons, it looks very much like the Franciscan (again) mission churches in New Mexico. Until now, no one has given an explanation for this transplant. If we consider that the Mexican churches are made of mud bricks, which explains the form and thickness of their walls and buttresses, the exact transplant of these forms into stone architecture, as is the case here, becomes even more inexplicable.

photo by Denis Roubien

Not far from Saint Francis, another mysterious spectacle: hiking from Falatados to Volax through Kathlikaros, we stumbled upon the church of the Assumption of the Virgin Mary, at the cemetery of Falatados. Below the bell tower we distinguished two mysterious figures, reminiscent of the pre-Columbian civilizations of America!

The bell tower of the Assumption of the Virgin Mary, at the cemetery of Falatados, with the mysterious figures reminiscent of the pre-Columbian civilizations of America

Natural particularities as well

And if you have had too much of culture, I have something different for you now, again unique, at least in Greece. I know, you are exasperated by so many unique things on this island. This last thing I will mention in the Inner Parts is a natural wonder. If you follow the trail from Falatados to Volax, you will arrive at an area full of thousands of round rocks.

The mysterious rocks at the trail from Falatados to Volax

Opinions differ as to their origin. Some experts say they were in the bottom of the sea when this area was immersed in Prehistoric times. Others say they are meteorites. Whichever is true, it's a sight you will not forget. Especially if you arrive at Volax (which actually means large pebble) and discover that its houses are built on some of these rocks, which stick out of their walls.

photo by Denis Roubien

Kardiani. First taste of the Outer Parts

And now to the Outer Parts...

We enter Kardiani at dusk. Kardiani is the first village one meets on the way from the Inner to the Outer Parts. So it seems to be the link between the two areas of Tinos. Here it's still green as in the Inner Parts. And very green at that. We haven't yet arrived at the marble areas, where vegetation is typically scarce.

Also the Baroque we saw in abundance in the Inner Parts still exists. And exactly here it makes its last appearance. And not just in the Catholic churches of Our Lady Kioura and the Assumption of the Virgin Mary, but also in the Orthodox church of the Holy Trinity. Because Kardiani constitutes a link from this point of view too. It's a mixed village, the only one in the Outer Parts with a Catholic population. So this is the last place of a strong Venetian imprint.

And since it's the last place, the imprint is intense. Therefore, the Baroque reigns in all three major churches. Perhaps it's the only village of Tinos with three large churches. All three facing the sea. Because Kardiani is one of the few villages that dared, in the age of piracy, be erected on the mountain brow and seen from the sea. Thanks to the courage of their ancestors, the modern inhabitants have the rare privilege of contemplating the sea from their homes.

311

Kardiani overlooking the sea, with its three major churches. In the front, Our Lady Kioura

Kardiani, Holy Trinity. While Orthodox, this one too is Baroque, like the other two

Kardiani, Holy Trinity. The curtain in the sanctuary is also made of marble!

But there is something that betrays that we got to the Outer Parts: marble. The marble façade and marble steeple of the Holy Trinity and the marble parts of Kioura worthily represent the local marble-sculpting tradition. Here begins Tinos of the artists.

It's Mrs Theresia who opens Our Lady Kioura for us. During the Venetian domination, Kioura-Kardiani (= Our Lady of hearts) was a pilgrimage of the whole Tinos. It gathered a large number of pilgrims, Catholic and Orthodox. Two shrines coexisted, one for each community.

Eventually, the church came to the Catholic community of the village of Kardiani, which had been built in the early 17th century. Therefore, but also due to the great distance that separated the area from all the other Catholic villages in the Inner Parts, the pilgrimage lost its general character.

The next day, when we go back, Mrs Theresia, faithful to the spirit of treats we also met in other villages, 'forces' us to empty a bag of chocolates. And when we leave, she asks with which ship we leave Tinos. And she promises to greet us with signals she will make to us with her 'little mirror'.

A characteristic imaginative Cydadic jardiniere in Kardiani

Kardiani, a sculpture of stone and lime

The bell tower of Our Lady Kioura. The Baroque apotheosis in Kardiani

Arriving at the first artistic centre. Ysternia

We say goodbye to Kardiani and reach Ysternia. Ysternia is another 'courageous' village overlooking the sea. And it's exactly from there that we come. We climbed from the Bight of Ysternia (Ormos Ysternion) through a paved trail made by unknown artists. Here we are in the Outer Parts for good. The Baroque ends, the vegetation diminishes and marble multiplies. But here the style is different.

Ysternia, Saint Paraskevi, with its imposing marble façade. The building that stands out in the village

As we said previously, in the Outer Parts, all villages except Kardiani are Orthodox. This region is the farthest from the administrative and economic centres of the island during the Venetian domination. So the Venetian imprint fades. Thus, the architecture is more familiar, reminding of other parts of Greece.

Except, of course, of the materials. Because the materials reveal another imprint: the imprint of Phidias. According to an ancient tradition, which is not absolutely certain, Phidias came from Tinos. It's possible that the tradition was created because of the marble quarries, which have been known since antiquity. Regardless of that, the many contemporary Phidias coming from the Outer Parts of Tinos justify the ancient tradition.

In the capital of the artists. Pyrgos, marble everywhere

After Ysternia, we reach Pyrgos, hiking from Venardados. Across the area, we see a number of 'katikies'. They are small constructions of dry stone, namely, without mortar. The farmers used them in times when travel was difficult. When they had a lot of work, they had no time to return to their village every night. So, they were staying here.

Pyrgos can claim the title of capital of the artists, being the birthplace of most of them. But it's also the birthplace of the one that many regard as the leading artist of modern Greece: Giannoulis Halepas (1851-1938).

Rightly, then, in Pyrgos is located the School of Marble Crafts, which worthily continues the tradition. From here come most of the marble craftsmen working in the restoration of ancient monuments. Their works above all in the Acropolis will convince you that they are absolutely worthy of their ancient colleagues.

Very naturally, then, Pyrgos is the marble village par excellence. There must be no other village in Greece with so much marble. The most impressive things we saw were the marble fountain in the main square, the churches of Saint Demetrios and Saint Nicholas and the funerary monuments in the cemetery.

'Katikies' outside Pyrgos

The œntral square of Pyrgos

The fountain in the central square of Pyrgos. Worthy of the village's tradition

photo by Denis Roubien

Unlike the Venetian semicircular skylights in the Inner Parts, here skylights are square and more recent

And of course, there are museums: the Museum of Tinian artists and the museum housed in the home of Halepas.

But the most unexpected is the intercity bus stop. Also, this is entirely made of marble. This must be an international originality.

Pyrgos. Probably the most beautiful bus stop in the world

But don't take the bus from the marble stop and leave Pyrgos yet. First, you must absolutely visit the amazing Museum of Marble Crafts outside the village. Not only it has very interesting exhibits and exemplary guided tour and audiovisual presentation of the techniques. But the building itself is a model of integration in a sensitive natural environment.

See you soon

Having visited the Outer Parts as well, we say goodbye to Tinos and sail towards Andros, with the port of Rafina as our final destination. And when the ship is off Kardiani, we look lest we distinguish the signals Mrs Theresia would make to us with her 'little mirror'.

And we see them. Only we wonder whether it's a little mirror or a full-length one. Did Mrs Theresia pull out her closet to make us signals with the door mirror? Because the signals are such that we are sure that they are visible from space. Even the aliens may discover Tinos. Who knows... Perhaps this way Tinos will add to its enthusiast fans some more, somewhat more distant...

ABOUT THE AUTHOR

Denis Roubien holds a PhD in Architectural History and is a professor in Higher Education and fervent cultural hiker. The hiking trips in which he participates, along with other travel experiences, are recorded in his books.

Thank you for reading this book. If you have the time, a review would be very helpful.

Printed in Great Britain
by Amazon